Stay Grateful!

Sheri Cole

Advance Praise

"Rooted to Rise *is a collection of real-life stories that portray the extraordinary way people mark our lives, from the family we're born into to the serendipitous collisions that shape us on our journey. You will laugh and cry and recognize yourself in what you read.*"

—**SALLY JENKINS**, *Washington Post* sports columnist, author, and Pulitzer Prize finalist

"*Al Davis, the former owner of the Oakland Raiders, would often tell me to watch this lady coach. She is brilliant. Davis, a true aficionado of women's basketball, was a Sherri Coale fan, so I followed his advice and started becoming one.* Rooted to Rise *is a powerful collection of stories written with a Joan Didion-like narrative that every coach, teacher, husband, and wife will benefit from reading. So thank you, Al, for the advice. Thank you more, Sherri, for the lessons.*"

—**MICHAEL LOMBARDI**, former General Manager and three-time Super Bowl-winning executive for the New England Patriots, San Francisco 49ers, Oakland Raiders, and Cleveland Browns

"Rooted to Rise *is a must-read for all coaches, leaders, teams, and anyone who wants to grow. Sherri shares the stories of pivotal moments in her life that helped her become one of the very best basketball coaches in the country. There's a reason we have had the successes we have had, and that's because of the people who have touched our lives. Sherri shares her people and encourages us to remember ours, and throughout the book, she shares so many incredible life lessons we all should insert into our own lives.*"

—**KEVIN EASTMAN**, former NBA coach, author, and executive coach

"Sherri is such a curious, driven, kind, and great-hearted leader. She has intentionally put her heart and soul into this book, Rooted to Rise. *Buy this book. Read this book! Your life and leadership will be better for it."*

—**RYAN HAWK**, author of *The Pursuit of Excellence and Welcome to Management* and host of *The Learning Leader Show*

"This eloquently written book of essays reveals the heart of a motivating coach and family-focused woman. Her ability to communicate her real-life experiences makes you feel as though you are present."

—**KRISTIN CHENOWETH**, Tony Award-winning actress

"One of the things I've always appreciated about Coach Coale has been her commitment to growing, learning, and improving. Our paths have crossed several times at retreats for coaches, and it was obvious that no matter how much she had already accomplished, she had an extraordinary drive to get better. It's pretty clear that Coach has always been on the lookout for a great lesson to carry with her into the locker room. In this book, she shares about the people and moments that inspired her throughout her tremendous career."

—**BRAD STEVENS**, President of Basketball Operations for the Boston Celtics

"I have enjoyed covering Oklahoma women's basketball for decades. Reading some of these behind-the-scenes stories was wonderful. If you are curious about what makes people great, this book is for you. It is a reminder of the power of sport and the people who shape the teams we love to cheer for."

—**HOLLY ROWE**, ESPN correspondent

THE REDWOOD LEGACIES
OF LIFE-ANCHORING PEOPLE

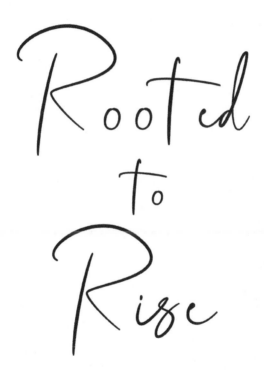

Rooted
to
Rise

SHERRI COALE

The following essays were originally published in slightly different form in the following publications:

"The Arm of His Chair" originally appeared digitally in Sherri's blog, "By the Weigh."

"Thin Air" originally appeared in ESPN the magazine.

Rooted to Rise
The Redwood Legacies of Life-Anchoring People

ISBN 978-1-5445-3264-6 Hardcover
       978-1-5445-3265-3 Paperback
       978-1-5445-3263-9 Ebook

For my mom,

who sees me, still, as I can be.

CONTENTS

INTRODUCTION. xiii

PART I

Shallow Roots

ENJOY THE VIEW. 3

SHOOTING STAR 5

PLATO ROAD 11

MORE THAN POTS AND PANS. 19

AT THE ARM OF HIS CHAIR 23

PART II

Goosepens

THE GIFT OF HARD 33

GYM RAT 39

THE ART OF ASKING 45

PAJAMA DAY 49

TO DRAW OR NOT TO DRAW 55

PART III

Rainmakers

LITTLE WILL 63

THIN AIR 69

WE CAN DO THIS 73

A STATELY OAK 79

"MY HEROES HAVE ALWAYS BEEN COWBOYS" 83

MINE WAS BORN LUCKY 87

THE BIG-TIME SMALL-COLLEGE COACH 93

TROUBLE 99

PART IV

Diverse Inhabitants

THE FOUNDATION 105

THE PINK LADDER 115

SPREADER OF JOY 119

THE PROTECTOR 131

OUR CANADIAN STAR 135

MASTER OF THE MARGINS 145

MS. MATTER-OF-FACT 153

THE GOLD BALL 159

ACKNOWLEDGMENTS 167

A FEW THINGS AT THE BEGINNING...

This collection of stories is in no way, shape, or form exhaustive. It would be impossible to write about all the impeccable people life has run me into. This is just a smattering, a snapshot of a few of the giant humans whose lives have tethered mine.

So, to my former players who aren't included here, take solace in the fact that neither is my mother, or my brother, or my husband. You're in the best of company uncaptured on these pages. As a matter of fact, you could look at it as though the best of the best got left out. I know you. You'll find a way to win.

To the gender sensitive: I use the word "guys" a lot when referring to my female players and even to groups of friends. It's a term of endearment, authentic to me, where I was raised, and the way I was taught the game. It just means "people" when I use it. Not men, not women, just people. And it is almost always in reference to people that I love.

INTRODUCTION

ALONG THE COAST OF CALIFORNIA, from Big Sur in the south to the Oregon border in the north, giant redwood trees hold hands underground.

You might think the towering redwoods would have roots that attach to the very core of the earth—deep, deep anchors that could support the giant mass that stands. But they don't. Their root systems are, ironically, quite shallow, reaching only from six to twelve feet under the ground, as their crowns soar so high you can scarcely see the top. Instead of growing down to find an anchor, redwood roots grow out…and wrap around each other.

They hold each other up.

So when the winds wail and the earth cracks, redwood trees stand. And they keep standing—sometimes for as long as 2,000 years. They survive and soar because of who they're growing beside. The underground entanglement not only holds them up; it supports them as they thrive.

People aren't much different. We don't become who we are on our own, and we sure don't stand without assistance. We are shaped and molded by those whose paths we cross. It's the intersection of our lives that makes us who we are.

We are grounded by others. We are fueled by others. We are elbow-locked with others as we reach and swell and grow.

This is a book about that: the impact of the tangly, life-anchoring connections that sustain us.

The stories in this book are about my people. But everybody has some.

I hope you recognize yours here.

PART I

Shallow Roots

"All this magnificence in height, and yet a
typical redwood's root system is only **6 to 12 feet deep**.
Redwoods create the strength to withstand powerful
winds and floods by extending their roots outwards,
up to 100 feet wide from the trunk, and living
in groves where their roots can intertwine."

—**"Climb a Coast Redwood," Sempervirens Fund**

"A tree with strong roots

laughs at storms."

—MALAY PROVERB

ENJOY THE VIEW

FALL WAS ALWAYS MY GRANNY'S favorite time of year. She loved it when the trees went to sleep green and woke up red and yellow. She loved the crisp air of an Oklahoma cold front and the onslaught of holidays that gave her an excuse to redecorate the house. Though I never heard her say it, I think what she loved above all else was the transition—the movement from one thing to another and the adrenalin that came with it. Being idle was *so* not her strong suit. My Granny loved to *go!* So when she went in the fall, we applauded a life lived extraordinarily well. And we all tried really hard not to be too sad, because she was headed to a better place, and she was always good at going. Plus, as God painted His world that October, she would never have wanted to obscure our view.

I love fall, too. I love my Japanese maples. I love my Chinese pistache. And I love my American mums. I love pulling in the driveway next to a carpet of green grass littered with leaves that looks like someone's bracelet just broke and scattered its jewels all across the lawn. The perfectly imperfect mess is glorious. When all the razzle dazzle of spring and summer fades away, we are left with one last *wow*. Autumn. It's like a giant graduation party. Then the world sheds its skin and becomes vulnerable again. How could one not love the promise of this time of year?

Though I'm all about things you can count on, I think one of the things I love most about fall is the unpredictability of it all. It's almost impossible to say when a tree is going to explode from the veins, or even if it will. Some years the trees that line my street look like they're on fire. And some years they just turn from green to tan. Some days the air is transparent, thin, and tight. And sometimes it's fog you can almost feel yourself disturbing as you move. You just never know. Nothing is sure but the winds of change.

The fall Granny left us was filled with change for my family and me. We were all still doing all the stuff we were supposed to do; we were just doing it with a giant hole in our hearts. Every tree that turned reminded me of Granny. For a few falls following her passing, I didn't decorate with pumpkins because that was Granny's job and joy. But every day I was thankful, even if my house didn't scream "Thanksgiving" from the windows and the doors.

I'm pretty sure I inherited her thirst for *go*. But especially that fall, I was reminded that the colors never last as long as we want them to. "Don't Blink," Kenny Chesney sings, because the years go faster than you think. Her ninety-two sure did.

SHOOTING STAR

MY PAPA WAS A FUNNY MAN. I write his name with two capital Ps because he wasn't a Papa, as in a distinguished father figure from a period novel. He was a Paw Paw, as in a small-town southern grandfather who would snatch your nose with sleight of hand, show it to you between his fingers, and then stick it back on the front of your face. That's how he said "Hello" and "I love you" and "Life is really good today, no matter what you might be thinking at this particular moment in time."

He whistled while he worked and while he didn't. He thumped high school boys on the back of the head, bought my brother and I potato chips and comic books at the local drugstore, and sat beside my Granny every Sunday morning at church. He was my hero before I realized what a hero was. And he was funny. I don't know if I've ever known anyone who loved to laugh more than him.

PaPa was a county deputy sheriff. Before that, he and Granny owned a mom-and-pop grocery store on Sinclair street in Healdton, Oklahoma. Before that, he was a farmer. But I only remember him as a man who wore a badge. I know he had a closet full of clothes, but I can't see him in my mind's eye in anything other than his perfectly pressed grays with a star pinned on his chest. Every morning he strapped on the shiny black-patent gun belt lined with bullets and a pearl-handled pistol. He'd don his cowboy hat—felt in the winter and straw in the summer—and head out to make his rounds. The drugstore for coffee, the Dairy Queen parking lot for speed patrol, the "Y" at Highway 70 for presence. PaPa didn't just do his job, he lived it. Everybody for miles around was glad he did.

Deputy cars come in all kinds of shapes and sizes. PaPa's office on wheels was a four-door Pontiac with star decals on the side that he drove like a snail up and down the streets of our sleepy rural town. *Hurry* wasn't a word he used, listened to, abided by, or even appeared to understand. He had a pace. He had a routine. He got there when he got there, which in retrospect seems like an Achilles heel for an officer of the law. Yet, steady and sure worked way better than fast for him. He was as predictable as the tick of a clock—except when he wasn't. That dichotomy made him real and rich and a shooting star of a man, even though that was never in a million years what he was trying to be.

Well before I was old enough to sit for my driver's license, I learned how to drive in PaPa's make-shift police car. We'd go out on the red-dirt back roads of Carter County, where he'd get out and amble around to the passenger side while I'd dead sprint and slide the corners to get under the wheel. (I did that every time. Not sure if I thought we were going to get caught or if I was afraid he might change his mind. Regardless, I vividly remember my heart and my feet racing to the driver's side.) And then he'd tell me nothing. Nothing.

With the scanner radio blaring charged chatter, I'd slip that cruiser into gear like I'd seen PaPa do hundreds of times, and I'd figure it out. I loved to drive, and he loved to let me. The days and the chughole roads taught me how. Driving was just one of the many things PaPa helped me learn.

PaPa had a few robust friendships and a million sanguine acquaintances. And he had a nickname for almost everybody. If you were "Goober Tom," you knew he liked you. If you were "Knothead," you knew you were doing something dumb. He weaved in and out of behavior shaping with a layman's genius, using language and laughter like a skilled artisan. PaPa nudged in the borders, like a collie herding cows, making better people at every turn.

One of the requirements of his position was to attend area high school sporting events—especially the emotionally charged rivalry games. He'd stand in the baseline corner of a sardine-packed gym, or slowly roam the deep end zone of an overflowing football field, and people would just behave better. While I'm certain the pearl-handled pistol at his waist had something to do with that, it wasn't so much the outfit as the way he wore it that kept the peace. Stationed beside his leg, I watched overtimes and flying dunks and touchdown dances and lobby fights. I saw the good, the bad, the ugly, the raw. I watched him work the shadows so those dancing in the lights could have their time. Hanging out with him was like scoring the golden Easter egg: I got to see both who and what I wanted to be when I grew up.

PaPa caught my softball pitches barehanded, rarely flinching no matter how hard I threw. He'd hit me pop flies and grounders, and he was always leaning on the fence just beyond the finish line of my quarter miles. He never told me to get outside and practice. He didn't coach my Little League teams. He didn't break down the game when I got home. But he loved to watch me play. Especially basketball. Even then it seemed he could sense what made my heart beat best.

Mostly, I walked to and from the gym that was only a couple of blocks from Granny and PaPa's house to practice basketball on my own. But sometimes, if it was getting dark or raining, PaPa would show up to give me a ride home. I never told him when I was going— we didn't keep a schedule on the wall. He just had a way of being there whether you knew you needed him or not. Nobody maneuvered the periphery quite like him.

The only time I remember PaPa ever saying anything to me—good or bad—about how I played the game was after one late-evening workout. A workout that consisted of me, a couple of balls, and an otherwise empty gym. The spot's still tender where his arrow stuck. It's funny—funny odd, not funny haha—how, looking back, I can't remember his words at all. I think he asked me a question, though I'm really not sure. And I'm super fuzzy on how I answered it if he did. Maybe I didn't—not out loud, anyway—but I still feel the point. Go to the gym to get better, or don't go at all. I'd been going through the motions and I knew it, and apparently so did he. No emotion, no judgment, no punishment to serve; just a well-aimed truth to the bullseye of my heart.

My precious PaPa died when I was a freshman in high school. He got sick fast and got bad faster. We came home from school, and the backdoor of the house was locked. We went to see him at Healdton Hospital. Then Ardmore Memorial Hospital. Each stay was brief and folded into the next at a more comprehensive spot. Within days, he was transferred to Mercy Hospital in Oklahoma City, where the room was pretty, quiet, and full of impending doom. I've visited hundreds of people at Mercy Hospital through the years, and it still hurts a little when I walk in the door. Loss is like that, I guess. The threshold never really heals entirely, even though you grow second skin all around it. Mercy Hospital's seventh floor is the last place I held his hand.

PaPa's passing kept tossing out lessons, just as his life had. I remember my mom's staunch bravery and her willingness to cry and admit how lost she felt saying goodbye to her Daddy. She was so elegantly brave that I assumed all who lost did so with grace and transparency. Now I know I was wrong. But what I saw in her was what he gave her: the strength to sit in grief and feel it, and then let it prompt her when it was time to move on.

I also remember my Granny's intense sadness, and what I learned from him through her as well. I remember asking Mom if Granny would ever be happy again. I was terrified this joyful hero of mine would forever and always be sad. Sitting on the flowered bedspread of Granny and PaPa's room, my mom said, "Yes, she'll be happy, but she probably won't ever be the same." That dart of truth scared me and emboldened me at the same time. That's when I realized that *happy* is a string that stretches through you, and when people you love die, they take some of you with them as they go.

At the funeral home in the days following PaPa's death, a steady stream of people passed through to pay their respects. There were extended family members, close friends, people from the community, brothers and sisters in Christ. But these streams were also dotted by people I had never seen. Some were dirty, some wore tattered clothes. Some had disheveled hair and smelled of alcohol. I was even scared of some. I didn't know them, and I didn't understand why they were there.

On the day of his service, the back three rows at the Shell Street Church of Christ were filled with those folks dotted between the familiar. When all was said and done, they lined up to see my Granny. Some said PaPa had given them food when they didn't have any; some said he had picked them up when they had no way to get where they needed to go; some said he had picked them up because they broke the law and handcuffed them and took them to jail.

PaPa was an 'all kinds of kinds' kind of guy. The lines he drew were straight, but the corners weren't sharp. I suspect that's why they all came to his celebration of life. He just had a way of stirring everything up—the good, the bad, the funny, the serious, the right, the wrong—he'd just knead it all with his big, strong hands, chuckle for a bit, and whistle as he went on his way. He could make good stuff out of anything. Maybe even me.

PLATO ROAD

THEY WERE ALREADY OLD when we were young. That created lots of space for assumptions, conclusions, and potentially inaccurate, though poetically licensed, connecting of dots by my brother and me. The DNA passes, though, even if it jumps over a big chasm to get there. The older we get, the more we see them in each other and ultimately in ourselves.

Grandma was German, and she had long, auburn hair that she braided and pinned up like a crown on the top of her head. She grayed around the front and the auburn had dulled over time, but her thick, wavy hair was long enough for her to sit on until the day she died. It was her signature. I learned how to braid standing behind her chair.

Grandpa was from Czechoslovakia, and he smoked a pipe. Unlike grandma, his hair was not his crowning glory, as he had very little. What he did have a lot of was strong opinions. He was smart in a kind of scary, intimidating way. Or maybe it wasn't his smartness as much as it was his size. He was a big man, a good 6' 4", which seemed gargantuan beside Grandma, who was maybe 5' 2" (and that was before age created a stoop). Nonetheless, I always felt the need to kind of cower around him. I think I got that from watching my dad.

The two, the German and the Czech, were quite a pair. When we went to their house to spend the weekend, cousins and relatives twice removed would always end up there, too. My dad was the youngest of ten, but the only child of Louis and Myra Buben. Grandpa had six children and Grandma had three, and when both of their spouses died, they found each other in Pennsylvania. Then they followed the railroad to Oklahoma, where they had my dad. Twelve people grew up in the two-story cottage bursting with independent air on the glorious lot at the corner of Plato Road.

Grandma had been a teacher in a one-room school. I guess that's how she was always able to corral the zoo that her house became on the weekends. She was like a sous chef and an air traffic controller at the same time. People did what they were supposed to around her— the gift of a teacher when no one's in school. Grandma never raised her voice, but it was obvious she was in charge. She was one of those people who thought way more than she spoke. I have to strain my brain to hear her voice now. I realize, looking back, that she saved it for when she actually had something to say. Brazen authenticity dripped off her, whether she was teaching me to count in German or how to knead the dough for bread. She was unapologetically herself in all things, in all ways, all the time. And she had a temper that went right along with the color of her hair.

Grandpa was a businessman. He was a high-ranking officer at Halliburton and an influential member of the community in the small southern Oklahoma town he chose as home. He was deeply involved in politics, he read voraciously, and he believed devoutly in God, though he and Grandma worshiped in slightly different ways. Their home was filled with stacks of *National Geographic* and *Reader's Digest*. Grandpa's study was wall-to-wall books. When the house filled up with relatives, I would claim my spot in his study, which flanked the family room to the north. The room was like a little space capsule filled with treasures that let me see a bigger world than the one I was in.

Grandma and Grandpa's house was Adventureland for my brother and me. For all my many cousins, really. The house on Plato Road was littered with unsolved riddles, its grounds fertile soil for imaginative minds. I think it's where we learned how not to be bored. We told horror stories in the basement alongside Grandma's canned vegetables, and busted up a good many shins and toes trying to escape up the stairs when it got too real. Getting accidentally locked in there by the tiny metal exterior hook was my greatest nightmare. I had a brother and a lot of older cousins. It happened more than once.

The house sat on a massive corner lot with enormous oak and cottonwood trees whose dispelled leaves piled around the house like snowdrifts in Montana. You literally could not get to the back door without plowing through the happenstance moat. Grandpa and Dad would often rake them into piles six feet high that would become anything and everything we wanted them to be. We'd dive into them as if they were a lake, hide inside of them as if they were our cocoon, and throw them to create a make-believe snowstorm. Saturday afternoons melted away with us in the belly of those piles of leaves. The fine dust would be in my hair, my eyes, my teeth, the crevices of my skin. Sometimes Dad would drag me out coughing and sneezing and begging not to have to go. They should put a price tag on the purity of happy that lives in a pile of leaves.

In the creek just off the kitchen, we fished for crawdads with bacon tied to a string. I learned the hard way how to hold them and what a good idea it was to wear shoes. There was a cellar door just off the porch—smooth metal that made a perfect slide, except on hot summer days, when it doubled as a griddle for bare legs that stuck instead of slid. In between the cellar and the creek was my kitchen: the place where I made mud pies and baked them in the sun, then decorated them with acorns and rocks and crumbled leaves. I displayed my creations for the family on a concrete retaining wall where I lined them all up like a fancy French bakery I had never seen. Grandma especially made me feel like it really mattered, what I'd done. I learned from her to notice what little people do.

Grandma and Grandpa's house bore rituals. Rituals of gathering, rituals of card games, rituals of food. We had beans and chili sauce (a special concoction you pour over brown beans, but it's not really chili at all). We had homemade bread and wilted lettuce salad. Fried potatoes with onions, served with pork chops and green beans that had been canned. We sucked on pork chop bones as a late-night snack and ate cold bacon in the afternoon. When we'd pack up to leave, Dad would have a brown sack full of chow chow, homemade jelly, cinnamon rolls, and made-by-hand bread. He was the baby, and Grandma catered to him even when he was grown. My brother and I were always glad she did.

Christmas was an event. Everyone came. The heartbeat of the tiny house reverberated through open windows and screen doors, the smell of all kinds of made-from-scratch food going with it. I think we drew names for gifts, but everybody did what they wanted. We had a crazy aunt whose children were long grown and gone, so she always bought gifts for all the kids. Trying to figure out what they were once we unwrapped them was our favorite part. I got an empty "Pet Rock" can one year. We laughed for hours, only because she thought it was so funny. I'm bumfuzzled by it still.

We had an uber-talented cousin who was musically trained and swam in an entirely different stream, and Grandpa always asked him to sing before we opened presents. We assumed it was because he was the only one in the house who could. When he'd begin to sing random songs no one knew the words to, we kids would bury our faces in pillows to muffle our laughter, while our ornery fathers wouldn't even try to hold it in. The Buben crowd was a tough one. Thin skin fell apart inside those walls. You'd better bring it or you wouldn't survive.

I only knew Grandpa as retired. As a fisherman, a gardener, a tender of the grapes. And as much as I suspected that there was a whole lot there inside this maestro of Christmas on Plato Road, I didn't really know about any of it until long after he had died. What I discovered through the years was that Grandpa was a leader and a thinker and a lover of words. He had a weekly column in the *Duncan Banner*—"Nebub's Needle"—where he expressed himself clearly and beautifully and lobbied hard for mutual understanding and for change, always courageously drawing a line across the sand. I went through boxes of his clippings at the house after Grandma died. Dad never wanted to read them or have much to do with what was left. I think not looking back was the only way he could carry on.

Grandma loved her garden, but as she got older, she couldn't physically tend to it as much as she would have liked. The front of her house always looked like a cover from *Better Homes and Gardens* magazine, though. Nature was putty in her hands. And as the years passed, she continued to read. Big print, then with a magnifying glass. For as long as I knew her, she read every single day. And she cooked and she gave me homemade bread for Christmas tied up by a red bow. She lived for two decades after Grandpa. Long enough to be a part of my wedding, play toy trucks with my son, and not quite long enough to hold my infant daughter in her hands. Grandma lived completely for three months shy of one hundred years.

My dad and his parents shared complicated relationships, the way most families do. But all the complicated shed like skin when it came time to say goodbye. Watching your parents lose theirs is cruel and unusual pain. But it teaches you a bit about grace. I grew up a lot by watching Dad watch his folks go.

Family is a crazy-quilt-like explanation for most of us: why we are who we are and how. No doubt a lot of me came from Plato Road. As a young adult, when I asked for a subscription to *Reader's Digest* for Christmas, everybody was pretty sure where that seed had been planted. And as I water my peonies, I know where that came from, too.

The cavernous age gap between Grandma and Grandpa and us prevented them from being playmates or buddies, like grandparents sometimes are. They were more like people we knew we were related to but had to get to know in their world. They were just too old to immerse themselves in ours. They couldn't come to our ballgames or recitals, and as a result, I have zero memories of them anywhere except the house on the glorious corner lot in Duncan, Oklahoma. But there's a kind of magic in the memory because of that. I see who they were and who I am, and it's clear that blood finds all kinds of ways to travel—across miles, across years—even in and out and around and through the people in between. But it gets there one way or another, and we carry it with us as we go.

MORE THAN POTS AND PANS

I CLEARLY REMEMBER the first time I figured out how good
it felt to set a goal and reach it. I was doing ball-handling drills in my
Granny's kitchen. Sounds odd, I know. But it was the perfect setup.
The room was laid out in the shape of a C, with the fridge anchoring
one end, and the stove anchoring the other. Connecting the two was
a string of durable white cabinets, interrupted only by a sink. The
floor was linoleum—white with little blue flowers in the corners of
every faux tile. And above the stove was a clock, a dime-store special
that had big black numbers and a second hand that plunked reliably
lap after lap. It was almost better than a gym.

It was there, in the heart of Granny's home, that I learned to
handle a basketball. Three times a day it was me, a scarred-up Voit,
and my red spiral notebook of drills and charts showing up to race
against the clock. I would pound the ball with my left hand until the
clock's lesser arrow lined up perfectly on twelve, and then I would
fly. For thirty seconds, or sometimes for sixty, I would wrap and slam
that ball in between and around my legs and body, counting every
turn. Three times a day, every day, all summer, I raced against time
until the ball was an extension of my hand.

That kitchen was a magical place. In addition to being a makeshift gym, it was, first and foremost, the birthplace of Granny's infamous mashed potatoes. Richer than dessert, they were a southern Oklahoma legend. If you didn't get in the front of the line on potluck Sundays, you weren't getting any. And once you had Granny's masterpiece, no other mashed potatoes on the planet would do. I have personally watched that concoction change the way a number of people see the world.

From this room with the rickety stove also came seas of meals for families in distress. Cupcakes multiplied there like loaves and fishes, and cookies went out by the truckload. Granny's tiny little space taught me that compassion has arms and hands, and that generosity has no price tag. When a need arose, we went to the kitchen to try to do something about it.

The kitchen was also a rural house of couture. Granny was widely known as one of the best seamstresses around, and most of her sewing took place right there in the same air where the ball bounced and the chicken fried. In the corner of the room, where the linoleum liked to curl up from the floor around the edges, sat an old Singer sewing machine that rarely rested. It produced bedspreads and curtains, slacks and jackets, Halloween costumes, and even a prom dress. I once made an aqua blue terry cloth cover-up for a home economics project there. I vividly remember chasing that crawly terry cloth fabric all around the room just to cut it. Granny watched, snickering to herself I am sure, but she never said a word. When I pulled the finished product off the machine and held it up for examination, it was large enough for both of us to wear together. We laughed until we cried. I learned then and there that thread can be ripped out and seams can be resewn and you can eventually get it right if it's important enough to you.

I swear, angels hovered in that room.

When I was in junior high, I participated in the Carter County Fair for no other reason than because our teacher required it, and the kitchen once again became the incubator. Some kids showed animals, some were involved in the Scouts, some did arts and crafts. Since sports wasn't an option, I chose baking, a category about three area codes outside of my comfort zone. However, since the kitchen was my spot, I figured the worst that could happen was that my dish would lose, and I could eat it. Plus, I had Granny for a teacher, so I figured success, though a definite long shot, would never be completely out of reach.

So I made a pecan roll. With Granny over my shoulder, I boiled and stirred and chopped and rolled and created this thing that looked kind of pretty and tasted even better, they said. I brought the remnants of it home in a box with a blue ribbon that said "Best in Show." My family had never been so surprised. We hung the ribbon on the kitchen wall next to the clock with big black numbers and the predictable second hand, and we laughed every time we walked by it for weeks. No way that happened without the karma of that kitchen, where dreams were born and given wings to fly.

Years later, when my PaPa died, I remember standing in the kitchen a lot. Especially the day of the funeral. That room just seemed safe. Looking back, I now know why. The story of my life was there.

I notice it still, the gravitational pull of the kitchen. When friends come to our house, no matter where the party starts, the kitchen is where we always end up. We've mended hearts while huddled on the counter, untangled messes while sitting on the brick paver floor, and created roads where there weren't any while leaning against the fridge. Our kitchen is where hard things get tackled and where big dreams get hatched, take root, and grow. Maybe it's the "possibility place" in every home. Or maybe it just seems sacred to me because I still feel Granny there. Either way, it's where our family's heart beats loudest—the avenue through which our house became our home. Such is the role of kitchen hubs that nourish both our bodies and our souls.

AT THE ARM OF HIS CHAIR

THE **"WAY BACK WHEN"** is like a series of little movies. The day I accidentally tripped the brake on the golf cart while Dad was standing over his ball on hole number thirteen. The day we drove that shiny midnight-blue Buick Regal off the lot and he taught me how to check the oil and work the jack. The day he walked me down the aisle, nervous as a cat, me in my veil, calming him and running the show as I suppose I have always been prone to do. But it's weird. Other than walking down the aisle, I don't remember him at all from that day. These little mini-movies work like that. I clearly remember him holding my firstborn. And the endless wrestling matches and Cowboy-and-Indians fights and fishing escapades with both of my kids. I remember the cartoon surprises that came in the mail addressed personally to each of them, and the closed-lip grin that stretched with pride when they made a tackle or hit a ball or walked into the room. And then it kind of stops. My memory train, that is. There's a hole in the middle.

The ending—the last six years—are vivid. Gnarly and almost too hot to touch. But they are my treasure, still. The day it hit me that he was gone and not coming back, I cleaned his house with a fury.

Alongside me were my closest friends, not saying much, just cleaning and carrying and sorting. Yeoman's work to tether me to what was still left. And I'm not talking about the house on Jon Street.

In the marrow of the dripping days when minutes felt like weeks, I would sit with him. I would consciously think, "Say something that matters. Draw him into conversation. Work harder to connect." Then I would stare at the TV with him and surrender. Being there was the best I could do at the time.

But I do feel bad about the middle.

The middle was what I missed. I was so busy raising my kids and working my job and living my life that I failed to pay attention. Weekly phone calls were blurs. And when he wouldn't answer, I got frustrated instead of concerned. When we visited and he seemed disengaged, I secretly assumed he had given in to his inner cynic, that he had chosen to withdraw, that he wasn't fighting for joy and purpose (as I, obviously, was). Self-righteousness is so easy to recognize in the rearview mirror. While he slipped off, I was looking the other way.

During those last six years, all I ever wanted was for him not to feel scared, which is a really odd thing for an achiever to have as a beacon because despite anyone's best efforts, that's as difficult to measure as it is to control. But that was my pipe dream. That's why my car drove to Brookdale Assisted Living Center, Walmart, and the VA Hospital at all hours of the day and night. I never wanted my Dad to be lonely or in pain or angry. But mostly I wanted him never to be scared.

Unfortunately—or maybe fortunately, as I think about it—I discovered that I didn't have that power. No matter how hard I tried.

The best I could do was make sure he felt loved. And I think I did that, to the best of my quart-sized capacity, I suppose. I remember sitting beside him searching for some sort of divergent question to pose that would send something—anything—back in my direction. For the last few years, trying to have a conversation was like playing tennis without a partner. When you hit the ball over the net, it never came back. I would beat myself over the head incessantly—I was a teacher, for God's sake! Why couldn't I come up with a good question? Surely something could elicit a response. But the harder I reached, the better the words hid. Over time, I surrendered to the silence, crossing my fingers that love would fill in the cracks. I hope Dad knows how much I learned sitting by the arm of his chair.

Parents teach in all kinds of ways. Dad was never much of a lecturer or a philosopher, or really much of a talker at all. But he was a laugher. And a face maker. And a farter. And a goofball. So far from perfect, we won't even go there. But I'm not so sure perfect is ever an admirable goal.

Dad did more than he said. He made forts and caves for my friends and me for weekend sleepovers, complete with hand-delivered popcorn and Hershey kisses. He made legendary Saturday morning breakfasts. He showed up at every game I ever played or coached if it was within his ability to get there. I tried hard on some of those silent visits at the assisted living center to remember him ever congratulating me for scoring a lot of points or making a big deal out of winning a big game, but I never could remember a time. The only thing I recall clearly is that he always looked at me the same regardless of the outcome. He loved it when we won and hated it when we lost, but he left the coaching to the coaches, and the outcome never surpassed the joy he got from watching me play. When the game was over, he'd grab me by the back of the neck with one hand and we'd go get a cheeseburger. While I cherish what he did, I equally value what he didn't do.

Dementia is a painful disease—they say more painful for the loved ones than the patient. But I'm not sure I buy that. I looked into his eyes. When he wasn't eating and I worried that he felt hungry, the doctors said that his brain probably didn't even connect the two. I can get on that channel, but lucidity is so fluid. I can't help but think there had to be seconds every now and then when a chili dog sounded like something he would trade breath for.

Nobody seems to understand the disease. It makes some people angry and others vile. It softens some and hardens others. It twists and torques the best and the worst of its victims—there's no predicting and even less explaining. It just kind of goes where it goes and takes the person we love with it. I still saw vintage Dad down to the last days. As his bones protruded, his muscles withered away, and his skin hung like a veil, I thought he had more Rocky in him than the world ever knew. He just wore it in his own way.

The last few years were like an electrocardiogram. Things would blip along monotonously and then there would be a spike. Usually when I went out of town. You could almost set your watch to it. I would get a call that he had fallen or had some sort of episode or there was an issue with his meds. It might be travel for work, perhaps for play; I might be across the state and I might be across the world. But it was like he knew. In the beginning, it made me so frustrated. After a while it made me mad. Then I turned smug. ("I knew this would happen! It always does!") My omniscience was arrogant and ugly, not to mention pathetic. A couple of years down the road, the whole scenario grew me grateful, because when I got the terror alert, at least I knew he was alive.

But the graph was always going. Blip, blip, blip, *bam*. In retrospect, the *bams*, for whatever reason, are burned in my brain like a brand. And lots of them make me laugh. Like the time I couldn't get him to let go of the walker to sit in his recliner. I would pry apart one grip and he would batten down the other, trapping my hand under his in the clutch. The cycle continued until my fingers were bruised and the back of my Sunday dress was soaked in sweat. This went on for A While. I think I finally leveraged my weight and chest-bumped him into the chair. I can still see the walker's legs parallel to the floor, positioned like the lion tamer's stool. What I remember most about it, though, is how hard we both laughed when it was over.

Conversely, some of the *bams* make me cry. Like the time we were sitting in the Brookdale lobby listening to a talented young man play the guitar and sing everything from funny folk songs to classic country. Though Dad couldn't sing along or tap his foot or clap to show appreciation, his eyes smiled and danced and he held on tight to my hand. The *bam* came with the finale. As the generous stranger played "Amazing Grace," my non-communicative dad mouthed every word. I'll never forget it as long as I live. I sang until I couldn't any longer, and then I just tried to absorb the seconds like a sponge. In Oklahoma, they always ask what you'd grab to take with you if a tornado was coming. If that memory was a thing, that would be what I'd clutch and run with.

The steady *blips*, though, really belonged to the nurses. I always felt like they gave him another life when he could no longer remember the one he used to have. If he had retained a decent level of health in his latter years and lived at home, he would have never received the kind of slathering love and attention he got from this crew. (What an upside-down silver lining. But it is, ironically, true.) I fed him when I visited—from big spoons, in the beginning, that I had to wrestle away from him when he wanted to go too fast—then from strategically bent spoons, when the highway from the bowl to the mouth got crooked; and finally from straws, first through his lips and then via the suction of my thumb. But they did it every day. The Angels of the Blips. I cut his hair and trimmed his mustache, but they cleaned and combed both with the regularity of a clock's tick. They did everything else that a daughter has a hard time doing, too. And I never saw them do anything they did without love. He felt it, too. If I hadn't been so grateful, I think I would have been jealous of the connection they shared.

When Dad finally gave up the ghost, his whole family was there. Kids and their spouses, grandkids, friends who were like family, caretakers who loved him desperately. Everybody. Except for me. Wouldn't you know it? I was in Phoenix, Arizona. Go figure. But it went down exactly the way it was supposed to go down, the way he had been preparing me for all along. We'd had our time, and he and I both knew I had always taken up too much room. The night before he passed, my twenty-one-year-old daughter slept in his hospital bed with him. I can only guess she did it because she loved him and because she knows that's what I would have done if I could have been there, and because she got his heart. My best friend stayed, too. She sat in the chair and snapped a picture of it all. It stays in my head, but if a storm were coming, that snapshot would go in the tornado bag, too.

We had a service void of pomp and based on circumstance because that's who Joe Buben was. He liked to slide in the side door and slip out the back. So we tried to celebrate his life in his fashion. We played the Platters in the beginning, "How Great is Our God" at the end, and "Amazing Grace" smack dab in the middle. My brother spoke like a champ, his words making those in the audience who didn't know our dad feel like they did, his poise and presence reflecting a father's life well lived. Dad would have been in awe, and his face would have turned predictably red. I pictured him standing in the back with his hands in his pockets, chin down, eyes and lips smiling to beat the band. That's how he looked when he was proud. He would have also wanted us to laugh and to find some things to make fun of, and he wouldn't have wanted us to be there very long. So we got in and got out and we hemmed his thirty minutes tightly in prayer.

But the service is just the suturing. It's what keeps you stitched together while you try to get on with things. And that's the tricky part.

My parents were divorced when I was young, and though Dad never lived more than five minutes away from us when I was growing up, visiting him was what I did. So we said goodbye a lot. Then I went off to college, got married, and had babies, and though the visits had more chunks of time in between them, they always ended the same: him standing in the front yard, waving goodbye.

He was never ready for me to leave, but he always let me go.

I'm sure when our car drove out of sight, he did what I'm doing now. He tried to pick up the place. So much stuff is left lying around after the wave. I awkwardly mess with it now, like a crooked drawer you can't get to close. And I laugh and cry in equal parts while I jiggle it. Just another thing I learned from my dad.

PART II

Goosepens

"Basal cavities are ubiquitous in coast redwood…
Known locally as 'goosepens', these basal hollows can be
large enough to hold livestock, as they did for early
Euro-American settlers. For centuries, large cavities
also provided the occasional shelter
for Native Americans."

—**"Coast Redwood Ecology and Management," Redwood**

"The true meaning of life

is to plant trees under whose shade

you do not expect to sit."

—NELSON HENDERSON

THE GIFT OF HARD

MIDDLE SCHOOL IS MESSY. Awkwardness is the norm, cool isn't even a possibility, and from those halls of dysfunction, high school looks like a dreamy place you see on TV. Ninth grade is the footbridge connecting the two. I had no more taken a step on that creaky wooden connector when my anything-but-cool freshman English teacher handed me a key to a door I didn't know existed.

Ms. Mitchell was . . . *different*, to be kind. *Odd* is probably a more accurate word. For starters, she was a Ms., and she was adamant about that. I didn't know what it meant, but her insistence on it made me know it mattered. She wore out-of-style clothes and boisterous jewelry, the likes of which made me think she had traveled, though her shoes made it clear she had not. Her charcoal-black hair was streaked with silver, and I never saw her without red or hot pink lipstick leaking just outside the boundaries that were supposed to contain it. I couldn't imagine where in our small town she might live, or how or why she got there in the first place.

I remember exactly where my desk was in her room, though—far wall, next to the windows, third row from the front. I remember the introductory hands-on tour she provided of our textbook. And I keenly remember what it smelled like to turn the pages as she talked. Ms. Mitchell's cardigan cape, no matter how primly draped, could not hide her brimming anticipation for the wild adventures we would go on through the written word. And I met her there despite all about her that I did not understand.

One day she kept me after class. She told me she wanted me to attend a statewide academic contest and take the English exam. She said it was different from many of the other subject areas because it required some outside reading. If I signed up, I would have to commit to the reading on my own time. I remember her seriousness and the challenge she laid down. I was flattered and a little scared, but there was no way I was saying no.

Two days later when I came to class, there was a fifty-cent paperback laying on my desk. It was a used copy of *The Pearl* by John Steinbeck. The corners of the cover were slightly curled, and I hadn't the slightest idea what it was about. All I knew was that it didn't look like anything I would have ever chosen in the library on my own. And though it read like Russian to me for a while, ultimately it introduced me to symbolism, personification, allegory, and theme. When I finished it, I had a different way of looking at the world.

I fell deeply and hopelessly in love. Not with Steinbeck, particularly, or with *The Pearl* specifically, but more so with the idea that books could be about so much more than the story they told. *The Pearl* made me think and scratch my head and stretch. I felt like I had wrestled a gorilla by the time I finished, but when I got there, it was as if someone had pulled the curtain back on "wow."

Ms. Mitchell propped open the door; the power of story invited me in.

Jolene Lewis, my senior English teacher, took the baton that Ms. Mitchell had handed me and ran with it. Mrs. Lewis was a tiny woman—she made me, at 5' 3", look tall—but she had a capacity that awed me. She also had a nasal southern drawl, a messy classroom, and a gaggle of kids—her own and the ones who flocked to her at Healdton High School. Mrs. Lewis did not give easy As. She did not tolerate fools. And she did not say things she didn't mean. That's why when she wrote in my yearbook that she expected to see a novel one day with my name scrawled across it, I believed it was only a matter of time.

If Ms. Mitchell gave me a ticket, Mrs. Lewis punched it. She carried compassion and self-deprecating humor like a country club lady carrying a designer bag. It made us all want to be like her, even if we didn't understand what it took to pull it off. While she never acted like an intellectual elite, I always knew she saw things most of the world missed. I took copious notes when she was teaching and eavesdropped like a spy when she wasn't. I adored her for being so normal and simultaneously so unlike anyone I had ever known. I wanted to write for her even if no one else ever read it.

So I went to college to play basketball and study English—unfortunately, pretty much in that order. At Oklahoma Christian University, my world continued to expand. The first book assigned by Peggy Gipson, my freshman English teacher, was *One Day in the Life of Ivan Denisovich*, by Alexander Solzhenitsyn. I was terrified simply by the names. But that book changed my view of time. It made me acutely aware of point of view. It inspired me to be tougher and wiser and made me feel so accomplished to have grown from a book most people couldn't even pronounce.

Then there was a poem called "The Naming of Parts" that I wrestled with and wrote about and dissected beyond recognition. It was like Pandora's box, full of surprise after surprise—symbolism gone mad in the guise of a gun. I inhaled Shakespeare's tragic *Troilus and Cressida*, stuttered through Chaucer's *Canterbury Tales* in its original Old English, and passionately stood up for *Hamlet's* Ophelia. Every hardback cover led to a rabbit hole I was happy to run through.

I could not get enough because of how much bigger the world was every time I finished a work. With each piece, I got better at grappling with form and function and language—though if I'm being honest, it never really got any easier. Teachers kept throwing out taller hurdles, posing tougher questions, holding up higher bars. The literary devices grew more complex, and the moral dilemmas of context more entrenched. Still, wild horses couldn't keep me out of the fray, for the gift of the struggle was worth it. What a view on the other side!

In the 1990s, actor Tom Hanks made a baseball movie called *A League of Their Own*. It was the story of an all-female traveling baseball team picking up the entertainment baton for men who were away at war. It was an anthem for women, its characters revealing all sides of the complex creatures we are. The slapstick, inflammatory style made us laugh, but the arc of the story made us bold. In the movie's most pivotal scene, Geena Davis, who plays Dottie, the tough-nosed, best player in the league, finally decides she's had enough. "I quit," she says. "It's just too hard." To which Tom Hanks, the sloppy chauvinistic manager who becomes their biggest fan, replies, "Too hard? Of course it's hard! If it wasn't, everybody would do it. It's the hard that makes it great."

That's exactly why I remember *The Pearl*. And Jolene Lewis. And Ivan Denisovich. It's why I appreciate the painful series of drafts it took to get me to an A on my first college research paper. I remember thinking Peggy Gipson must surely be the shrew Shakespeare was speaking of taming, but I eventually discovered she wasn't. She was just the wall I had to run through to be able to see.

Great teachers do that. They crack open a door and cue the siren's song that lures you in. Once inside, they give you *hard*. And then they let you decide what to do about it. I live indebted to them for the view.

GYM RAT

HE WAS A BALL COACH. The way he walked was a dead giveaway. So was his raspy voice and the way he wore his cap.

There were a lot of things he wasn't, but he was one of the best I've ever seen at being exactly who he was. And who he was was a gym rat—a guy who never got enough of a bouncing leather ball. Dan Hays was a purist, his being so ingrained in the game that it would be hard to tell who he might be without it. Even his grandkids called him Coach. He liked Motown, college football and baseball, playing tennis, and messing around with golf, but he was a man of few true loves. God, family, and the beat of a bouncing ball were his triumvirate, with very little space in between. Coach was lord of the gym where he lived, and legions of ballers, including me, grew up in his kingdom. I always felt like I got a leg up in that regard—like I got lucky and landed the silver spoon.

I met Dan Hays in The Nest (the main basketball gym on campus) on my first trip to Oklahoma Christian University, and I quickly learned it would be hard to ever go there and him not be around. He got there early. He stayed late. He taught the hungry, the talented, and the never-will-be. Coach was a custodian, an ever-present keeper of the space and the dreamers who inhabited it. He painted walls when they grew dingy, rehung nets when they got worn, and swept and swept and swept the floor. The gym was his palace, and he took care of it and the people who came there as if they were his own.

He had rules about being there, too. I always thought they weirdly mirrored what the Bible taught about church: all are welcome, consistent attendance is expected, and everybody's supposed to use their gifts no matter what they are. In his Nest, I never saw anyone turned away, regardless of skill set.

Coach made basketball the sport of choice for everyone on Oklahoma Christian's campus. Rarely was a gym without the echo of a bouncing ball. Students flocked to watch the men's and women's teams play competitively, and intramural tournaments filled the nights when intercollegiate competition wasn't going on. It was as if Coach doused the place in honey and everybody wanted a taste. Even faculty and staff made an ant trail to the Nest. With knee braces and elbow sleeves, professors and staff limped their way up and down the court on weekdays at noon. The infamous "noon leaguers" sweated and competed as if their lives depended on who had the most points at the end. I used to giggle watching such godly men play so poorly and get so angry when things didn't go their way. Such was the Dan Hays Law of the Gym: have fun, but throw your heart in. The more you give the game, the more it gives you in return.

Coach believed that anybody could improve and that everybody had a place in the game. Because of that perspective, he was a magnet for people who couldn't find a puzzle where they fit. His gym doors were always open, and all levels of prospective players came, like wanna-be knights in search of the Holy Grail. But Coach was also the guru that the best of the best sought out when they wanted to be better at the game they loved. He was a refiner, a polisher, a guy who could make you better at what you already did well. He was also known as the fixer, the go-to shot doctor who players from everywhere flocked to when the ball just wouldn't go in. Coach could fix a shot if it was broken, and if it wasn't, he'd fix what was. Tinkering was one of his skill sets, and he was never off the clock.

Coach was my teacher before he became my mentor. The summer prior to my freshman year, I came to the Oklahoma Christian campus to attend Cage Camp with the boys, in hopes of learning how to play defense (a skill my basketball experience had yet to teach me, as I'd grown up in small-town Oklahoma playing offense only in the six-on-six game.) At camp, under Coach's tutelage, I learned how to close-out, jump to the ball, and help the helper on the backside. The way he taught team defense made perfect sense to me. The how, the why, the what, the when. It just worked inside my brain. And while I'd long loved the ball and the skill and the very personal way you could get good at the game, I quickly realized that I loved how it all fit together just as much. If not even more. Clearly, Coach Hays was the pied piper who could take me to the promised land of coaching, where I so wanted to go.

Under his direction, I quickly became enamored with the angles and spacing and rhythm of basketball. I discovered I could not only understand the game, I could feel it. I could see the nuances, tap my foot to the beat. And little gave me more pleasure than watching the intricate choreography of players on the floor when they were getting it done. Coach Hays became my professor in a classroom called the gym. He taught hoops appreciation 24/7, and though it never showed up on my transcript, what I learned there was the foundation on which I built my career.

Coach also taught a cataloged course—one you actually received credit for—Theory of Coaching Basketball. I took that one my freshman year, and learned how to diagram plays, develop a scouting report for opponents, and get into almost any game for free. Coach taught us integral details about foundational offenses like Flex and the Triangle. I learned about George Mikan and his drill, about Jack Sikma and his move. And I learned that when you just keep digging, the game will teach you things you weren't even aware you needed to know.

Coach was a fundamentalist. A devout disciplinarian. A technical tactician and a stubborn builder of people who also felt the pull of the game. I was a courtside sponge. I watched him teach and push and pull and drive, rarely running out of patience or juice. He loved his protégés and felt the responsibilities of a teacher both inside and outside the lines, but as much as he loved the people who played it and hungered to learn it, his heart belonged to the game. It was his first and fiercest love.

Coach found his sweet spot early in life. He was as good as anybody who ever coached the game of basketball, and yet he spent his entire career at the National Association of Intercollegiate Athletics (NAIA) level, never succumbing to the bright lights and hefty paychecks of big-time ball. He would have choked on the limited access to players legislated by the next level, and he would have felt buried alive by all the external requirements layered on top of the game. Dan Hays knew that in his bones. He was a gym rat at his core, so he stayed in the lane where he could breathe best, with a broom in one hand and a ball in the other, paying reverence to the game.

THE ART OF ASKING

I TOOK A SHAKESPEARE COURSE in college. Our class met in a kind of long, rectangular, nondescript classroom on the top floor of the library building. It was a handful of upperclassmen—mostly English majors, though not necessarily English Education majors—and me. Our Shakespearean textbook was an enormous red hardback with print smaller than the type in my King James Bible. Reading one page was a job. I remember being terrified from the outset that I would have trouble keeping up.

The reading assignments were massive and the thinking even harder, but I never missed a class. We didn't have quizzes. The professor didn't take roll. But I couldn't not go, because magic happened there every day at 3:00 p.m.

And how it happened shaped my life as a learner and a teacher.

I remember the room having an extra-long chalkboard, almost as long as the wall. Most days, it had absolutely nothing on it. Some days, Dr. Darryl Tippens would stride in and whip a question across it. Or maybe a statement. Or maybe he'd just jot down a few phrases or ideas in a cluster for exploration. Then he'd perch on the edge of the table, swing one leg, and let us talk.

I walked out every day thinking I had never met a more brilliant man.

And he *was* pretty smart. In fact, he was a scholar. A guy who'd read more Shakespeare than most fanatics ever would, the kind of instructor who knew not just what he was teaching but where it came from, and why, and how. I admired all he knew, but I admired what he did with it even more.

I don't remember Dr. Tippens ever telling us anything: what we should think about a scene, how we should feel about a character, why one word was used instead of another. He just picked the threads of our thought patterns like my Granny used to pick the stitches when she let out seams. And given the room, his classroom of vagrant becomers grew.

I'm certain there were lots of times he ignited the conversation. And I'm sure he gently steered when we got caught in the whirlpool of what we couldn't know. But all I really remember are the nudges. The figurative elbow to the ribs when we weren't digging deep enough, or the pregnant air he held after one of us finished a thought. He didn't tell us what we needed to know; he let us find it. And he kept the air so charged that we wouldn't quit until we did.

Socrates would have been so proud of the professor's perfectly pressurized cocoon.

I learned more about how to think in Dr. Tippens's class than I did about Shakespeare, but I haven't forgotten much about either. That's the magic of the method. As we searched and stretched for understanding, we built ruts to be reused. His questioning and blatant unwillingness to give us the answers made us work for our conclusions. The process and the product stayed with us. We learned that what we strain for, sticks.

I took the skill of questioning into my gym as a coach, asking players what they noticed, what they discovered, how it felt, and why they did what they did. My goal was to expose the holes in their thinking without telling them where they were.

But this is not a natural road for a coach. Coaches are, by trade, extraordinary tellers. About as good as it gets when it comes to feeding with spoons. "Put your left foot here, put your right hand there." Do this and do that and do it just the way I tell you it needs to be done. That's how you build a muscle memory pattern, and it's an important part of physical performance, regardless of the field of play. But so is thinking and decision-making and figuring out what you believe to be true. All are necessary cogs of competition whose spoils linger far after the game is played.

Sometimes, while patiently waiting as my players squirmed under the subtle press of a question that had no right answer, I would think of Dr. Tippens and grin. I think he'd like the fact that young minds were having to reach for what they thought and hunt for what they knew.

And sometimes I'd sit on the edge of the scorer's table and swing one leg in his honor.

PAJAMA DAY

WHEN LITTLE PEOPLE GO TO big schools, it can be scary. Mostly for a little person's mom. When I took my firstborn to his first day of school, I recorded a grand video of his timid entrance on my Channel 5-sized video camera. I can close my eyes still and see his pensive face resting in his hand at his desk as he seemed to be taking stock of the whole wide world he'd entered and all the new people in it.

When I took my daughter four years later, it was different. She didn't want me tagging along, much less capturing video. "You are *not* going in with me," she announced when we pulled into the school parking lot. As a result, I have no video and no pictures of her historic day.

He wasn't sure about the world; she had already decided she owned it. Imagine being the kindergarten teacher standing in front of sixteen souls as widely different as my two on their first days of school.

We act like a teacher's job is to hold a goal post and bark out plays so that miniature people in progress can move the ball down the field—and I guess part of it is. But not all of it. Not even most of it, if we're really talking real. You can't write down what a teacher does any more than you can measure her by what her students do or do not do. Her job is so much bigger than that. A teacher's job is to tread water while juggling bowling pins and balancing a plate on her head in the middle of drawing geometry on the board with her toes. She's always in the water—on the clock or not—trained to be on high alert for moments when she can save or make a life. For a teacher, there's rarely a shore in sight.

My son's kindergarten teacher was a jolly Lilliputian who talked crazy fast and with her hands. She herded kids with giggles and celebrated them with smiles. It would be so easy to miss her brilliance. Her classroom, like most kindergarten workshops, oozed with interesting stuff. Kid creations. Learning tools. Wiggly, sweaty, wormy little humans. Mrs. Etter's room was a petri dish. From the ones bouncing off the walls to the ones sitting in the corner—and my son, who was somewhere in between—she had the pulse of it all, which she carried, gently, in the palm of her hand.

One nondescript day deep into the fall of my son's first year, I came home from work to discover that tomorrow was Pajama Day at school. Mrs. Etter had told them so, and Colton was juiced. As we got ready to read a story before bed, he laid out his favorite pair of PJs, excited as could be about whatever kind of magic tomorrow surely held.

My stomach itched.

I felt like I should have seen this coming. I prided myself on being so in tune. How had I missed such an important rite of passage as a theme day in my son's first semester of his first year of school?

Mortified isn't too strong of a word (young mothers exist in extremes) for the way I felt. So after I tucked him in, I went straight to our Thursday Folder, the place where all things pertaining to school came home with kids on a weekly basis. I unfolded every paper. I read all the smallest print. I found nothing anywhere about Pajama Day.

The next morning Colt bounced in for breakfast dressed in Spider-Man and ready to seize the day. I asked him if he was sure today was the day. I told him I hadn't found anything about Pajama Day in the Thursday folder. I asked again why he was so convinced.

"Because Mrs. Etter said," he said.

And that was that.

So we loaded up for school, me feeling like a disengaged and inattentive mom. (How do you not know about Pajama Day? How do you not participate in the build up? Maybe go together to buy a cool pair of PJs, make a plan for a get-up that's cooler than cool?) Apparently, in my busy-working-mom-life, I had missed Pajama Day. Translation: I sucked.

Through the cloud of guilt I drove, ultimately pulling into the drop-off line that snaked around the parking lot at the school. As we inched along, it occurred to me that none of the kids slamming car doors and running to the building had on PJs. About three cars back from the front, I asked Colton, my heart so tender in that spot still, "Are you sure it's Pajama Day?" He was undaunted. "It's Pajama Day, Mom. Mrs. Etter said."

And so I kissed him, told him to have a great day, and convinced myself it was a kindergarten thing, not a school-wide thing. Then I drove away like a turtle, terrified I'd just let my son walk off a cliff with no wings. I couldn't shake the dome of dread. His little five-year-old heart had only a few scabs and even fewer scars. If this turned out the way I feared it might, this one might leave a mark.

I kept waiting for a call from the school all morning long. I imagined getting it, rushing home to get regular clothes, and running them to the school in a bag. I could fix it. I could save him. I knew I could. But the call never came.

By the time noon rolled around (release time for half-day kindergarten), I was breathless with anticipation. I couldn't wait to hear about the day. Unfortunately, as I inched my way through the pick-up line, I realized my gut had been right all along. It wasn't a kindergarten thing. No other five-year-olds were coming to their parents' cars with their backpacks and lunchboxes and pajamas on. No one. Not one child. My heart was on the floorboard.

As I pulled up to the pick-up spot, Mrs. Etter came walking toward the car with Colton, he in Spider-Man and she in bunny slippers. He climbed in as undaunted as he'd climbed out four long hours ago. She was smiling her everyday grin.

"Was it Pajama Day?" I asked.

"It was," she said. "Colton is such a great listener. I reminded everyone yesterday and he was the only one who paid close enough attention to catch it. So he was our superhero leader today. You should be so proud of him! I know I sure am."

We exchanged smiles, heaped on a bit more praise, and I roughed up his hair. With a quick wave, we pulled away.

Mrs. Etter called me later. She said she had announced Pajama Day the day before and urged everyone to be sure and join in. She later realized she had confused her days, jumped a week ahead, and gave a directive that wasn't true. Most kids aren't listening at the end of the day anyway, so it didn't cross her mind again—until Spider-Man walked in the room that morning.

Mrs. Etter had a moment to throw a lifeline.

And she did.

She got her bunny slippers out of the closet and crowned Colton king for the day, so instead of a goat, a hero was made. Oh, the little big things teachers do.

Mrs. Etter apologized profusely, though I refused to take it. I told her this would be what I'd remember long after the schooling was done. Then I sniffled gratitude for this brilliant tiny woman who could pivot on a dime to steer a life, and did.

TO DRAW
OR NOT TO DRAW

MY DAD COULD REALLY DRAW. He worked in the oil and gas world, but that was just how the bills got paid. On the side, he painted signs for money, as lettering was his sweet spot. Almost every small business in our rural Oklahoma town had Dad's handiwork on its welcome board. While painting gave him great enjoyment and padded where the ends wouldn't meet, his passion was a pencil and pad.

Dad drew everything. Funny cartoons, landscapes, birds, a portrait of his parents. The pencil was a magical wand when tucked between the thumb and index finger of his right hand. I used to sit in his lap and tell him things to draw. I never came up with anything he couldn't make look real, or at least really funny. He was an untrained artisan who had hitchhiked home from college to join the National Guard and find a way to get by. Somewhere along the way, and maybe long before, he discovered he could draw…though I always wondered if he understood how well. I used to try to be just like him with only drippings from his gift.

When I was in the first grade, I entered a contest to make a poster about poison control. I went with a pencil sketch, of course. My game plan was to draw a boy sitting cross-legged with drug vials and pill bottles littered around him. The caption had something to do with keeping medications safely out of the reach of children, but I honestly can't remember what the contest was about or even why I was in it. I just remember that I won. And that there was a lot of whispering.

Dad had helped me with the concept, the spacing, and the layout of the sketch. I knew how to measure and align and did so with precision, the way I'd watched him do incessantly across the sawhorses in his barn. It was a poster for a silly contest at school, but I attacked it the only way I knew how—with every fiber of my being. It was toil with my tongue hanging out the side of my mouth. The lettering came pretty easily, but I worked and worked and worked at the details of the boy. I vividly remember struggling with the lines of his limbs, in disbelief at how hard it was to draw bent arms and legs. I sketched softly and erased a lot.

When judgment day came, my poster had a big blue ribbon hanging on its corner. I had no idea that's what happened when your art was picked as the best, or what it would feel like to win. I don't think I had even thought winning was an option when I entered, so the spoils came from left field, and when they landed in my lap, it felt like I had caught a cloud. I knew immediately that earning wins was something I would always want to do.

My first grade teacher, Mrs. Lucille Hughes, was a legend at Sunset Elementary. She was the golden standard if ever there was one. Mrs.

Hughes had back-combed hair and cat-eye glasses that hung from a chain around her neck when they weren't sitting on her nose. She was Charles in Charge—a printing press for miniature humans who sat up straight and colored neatly inside the lines. She and the plastic ruler she carried made sure of that. Her track record was renowned. I attended holiday parties in her classroom with my Granny when I was three and my brother was in first grade, and everyone I knew had had her as a teacher—she had even taught my mom. When I turned six and was assigned to Mrs. Hughes's classroom, I thought I'd roped the moon.

A few days after my blue ribbon victory, Mrs. Hughes handed out the morning's assignments and then motioned for me to join her at the back of the room. There I found a piece of white poster board, a ruler, some pencils, and ample room to work. She seemed a little nervous, and I was very confused. She had some news to break, that much was obvious. The bush she was beating around didn't hide her very well.

She told me we needed to draw another poster. "Huh?" I'm sure I said. It needed to be just like the one in the contest, "exactly," as a matter of fact, she explained. I couldn't imagine anyone having any need for two "don't do poison" posters, so I innocently asked her to help me understand why. I cried as she started to talk.

She said there had been some grumbling; among whom, she was not inclined to say. But some folks seemed to think that I didn't draw the boy on the poster. They felt like it was a bit too accurate for a six-year-old's skill. It was a small town; most people knew how my dad could draw. So Mrs. Hughes was bound and determined to prove them wrong. However, I did not want to play.

She said I could work on it during school, and she'd be the witness that every line of it was mine. I respectfully declined. I didn't want to draw anymore. It was hard enough the first time; I was sick and tired of rearranging tiny lead lines. And suddenly it wasn't much fun to win anymore, either.

But Mrs. Hughes wasn't having any of it. She handed me the pencil and said, "Draw." Then she dropped off a box of Kleenex for my snot and went back to the front of the room to teach. I sat on the floor with my blank canvas and the slivers of glass that surround you when your innocence gets smashed. More than anything, I did not want to draw.

Yet I did. Timidly at first, so distracted by the thousands of thoughts darting through my head. Then more focused but mightily frustrated as I fell back into the same ruts of difficulty I got stuck in the first time around. Those arms, and those crossed legs! Yet I drew... bravely, almost in defiance of those who had second-guessed. I had something to prove, and I had a dad to protect. My integrity was not on the chopping block alone; his was there, too.

A few days later, when I finally finished the poster, the local paper came to take a picture. Granny curled my bangs and laid out my favorite low-waisted, striped dress and black patent shoes for the occasion. Mrs. Hughes let them take a picture of her and me and the work, but then she demanded that they take one of me on the floor next to the poster with a pencil in my hand. My first grade teacher wanted documentation of what she had watched me do.

I suppose the world was appeased, but it never mattered very much to me after that—the world's opinion, that is. But I'll tell you what did matter: the fight in my first grade teacher's eyes. She hadn't taken up for me; she had built me a one-way road to take up for myself. By turning my shoulders in the right direction, pushing me forward, and then walking away, she taught me how to be tough. She taught me to hang my hat on what I did, not what others thought about it, good or bad. And she taught me that leaders stand up for what they believe in and fight for the rights of those in their care.

I got a lesson that wasn't in the textbook. First grade not only prepared me for second, it laid a nonporous foundation for life beyond the fences of a school. It was a gift I tried relentlessly to repay to Lucille Hughes between the day she retired and the day the good Lord came to get her. It never happened, though. The only way to settle a score that fundamental is to pass it on.

PART III

Rainmakers

"Redwoods need massive amounts of water to survive—according to one report, as much as 600 quarts of water each day. To make it through the summer dry season, redwoods make their own rain, getting 15 to 45% of their water directly from coastal fog, which they are able to capture from the air thanks to specially shaped branches and leaves.

Think of redwoods like giant fog receptors. As the fog rolls in, the moisture condenses on the leaves and drips down to nourish the tree's roots and the plant communities below. On especially foggy days, it can almost look like it's raining underneath a redwood canopy. And fog has the added bonus of reducing evaporation, making it easier for the trees to hold onto their water in the heat of the summer."

—Justin Garland, Open Space Trust

"There are rich counsels in the trees."

—HERBERT P. HORNE

LITTLE WILL

"**LOOK OUT! I'M COMIN' THROUGH!**" I heard him before I saw him. When I first met Little Will, he was driving a Big Wheel through the corridors of Children's Hospital. And he was locked in. If you were in his path, too bad. He had warned you. Everybody and everything was fair game.

I immediately thought he must be a cancer patient's little brother, occupying time while a sibling endured chemo or a gaggle of doctors invaded the room. But his blazing bald head gave him away.

Unfortunately, Little Will was a regular. He owned the tenth floor.

Will loved toy cars—he had dozens—and his favorites were police cars, of which he had two. He'd drive his fleet for hours on end, over the food tray that stretched across his bed, under the pillows he would pile to make a cave, through the sheets and blankets and bars and tubes and bags. Will turned the common into the exceptional. That was his M.O. Little Will would always find a way.

Will was diagnosed with acute lymphoblastic leukemia, or ALL, when he was two years old. Brilliant doctors and magical medicines gave him bouts of normalcy, but the devilish disease just kept popping back up, requiring him to spend the majority of his childhood on the tenth floor of Children's Hospital in Oklahoma City.

One day after the first of the year, on one of our team's regular trips to Children's, my guys got to meet this little fireball. He bounced into the lobby wearing a grin that dwarfed his face while tugging up his too-long, too-big jeans. One of our players asked him what his name was, to which he replied, "William Burgess the third, but you can just call me Little Will if you want." Talk about having the room at *hello*.

That day in the lobby of Children's Hospital, Will held court. All of the kids from the hematology/oncology unit and our players filmed a music video to Sara Bareilles's "Brave," and Will was happy to play a part, but he had no time for retakes or do-overs. The pursuit of perfection didn't much interest him. He had way too much to do.

Something about being seven and having lived 61,320 hours—never knowing whether or not any given one is your last—gives you the chutzpah to cut through the crap. Will lived an unapologetically candid life. He told the pretty girls they were pretty, and if he didn't like a song, he didn't sing it. I never heard him be negative or even naively mean as little kids can sometimes be. He just gravitated toward the good, and there didn't seem to be any space left for anything else. He hugged and he held your hand and he snuggled and he laughed. What he did not do was squander time. His tolerance level for hand-wringing and whining was a big fat zero. Even though he was just a kid, I think he innately knew he just didn't have any minutes to spare, so he opened the floodgates and let all of himself out.

If you were within shouting distance, you got him all over you. There just wasn't any way around it.

We made party hats that day in the oncology lobby, and we had puppet shows, but the gem of the day was a game of "Duck Duck Goose" that just sort of rose organically from the chaos. Kind of like the box the toys came in at Christmas, the children flocked to it. And William Burgess III became the star of the show.

When tapped on the head, Will chased with zest. When selecting his next target, Will chose with style. And yet, quickly, almost as quickly as he taught the circle how the game was to be played, Will slid to the center of it and asked to pass on getting picked.

Maybe he was tired. I watched him intently, though, and it didn't appear that he was. Maybe the running made him sick or it was painful, though I couldn't discern either as he motored around the group. I remember the game continuing—Nicole diving to tag kids, Maddie getting tackled (who cares if she has on a knee brace!), KK pretending to be lost so the little girl one-eighth her size could catch her—it all carried on in the direction Will had sent it. But it was blurry to me. I was mesmerized by the little man in the middle.

Will sat in the heart of the group with his legs crossed, one arm wrapped around and through Morgan's and the other arm clinging to Aaryn's like a vine. I swear if someone had turned off the lights, you would've seen him glow. As the ducks and the geese chased one another around the room, the circle grew consistently more misshapen, for Will just kept collecting people in the middle.

Then it occurred to me why he'd passed on getting picked: he didn't want to be the one it was all about. Will wanted to be all about *it*. He wanted the simple merriment of it all to wash over him. He wanted the best seat in the house, the spot from which he wouldn't miss a thing.

Our players didn't know it until later, but that very day Will had been re-admitted to the hospital and told that his cancer was back. Again. This was the third time. And when you're seven, strike three almost always means you're out.

Our team was devastated. A group of them made a pact to go visit regularly, and they held it as if they'd signed it in blood. They made him Valentines and took him pictures in frames. They played cars and video games, and they climbed onto his bed like he told them to because making Will happy made everything in the world seem right. One look at his smiling face, and it was hard to imagine anything anywhere being wrong. Even basketball games, the apex of our measured worlds, became tiny little blips on the radar screen of life. Will exuded a healing salve that masked his own and everyone else's pain.

Some days, the visits were rough. As the disease ravaged on, he choked a lot. He rarely ate. And he slept more and more and more. Our players' schedules were packed; our season was taxing, to say the least, but you couldn't talk them out of going to see him. They had taken on Will's bravado. They would not be denied.

On February 28, 2014, William Burgess III went to Heaven. We were on the road, so I told our guys at our team meeting in the hotel ballroom, and then I led them in a sob-filled prayer. From that point forward, some players wrote "Lil Will" on their tape; some wrote it on their shoes. The regularly visiting troopers made the trek to eastern Oklahoma to his memorial service. I was so unbelievably proud of our guys' compassion and their commitment to Will, I almost burst at the seams. I wanted the world to know what special souls they were.

More than anything, I wanted them to play like he lived.

Little Will taught all who knew him about resilience. He was a walking, talking, living, breathing ball of Silly Putty™. He bounced back every time. And he modeled toughness and joy and gratitude and fight. He was, in so many perfect ways, all any of us ever want our teams to be.

But our crew couldn't do it. They couldn't quite play like he lived.

I think some of them tried. I think some of them even thought they did. But they didn't, and it haunted me. It haunted me because more than anything, I wanted there to be a reason. I wanted Will's falling star of a life to have a palpable purpose for my guys. I wanted the awful real-life suffering of an innocent kid to be the impetus for a fairy tale. I wanted all of it—his too-brief existence and our too-shallow performances—to make some kind of sense.

What I loved most about Will was that he lived with the floodgates open. Ironically, that's the part our team could never get. Will infected you. He wasn't perfect. But he was real, and you became your best self around him because of it.

One of my Achilles heels as a coach is that I always want the package tied up in a bow. I want seasons to become Hollywood movies. I want everybody to get it—now.

Unfortunately, that rarely happens.

But what keeps me plugging along is this: infections sometimes lay dormant for a long, long time. One may be in you without you even knowing that you have it. And then one random day, it just takes over, and you can't hide it anymore. That's what I'm banking on with Will. I hope he spreads through everyone who ever knew him and that none of us ever recover.

THIN AIR

WHEN I FIRST MET Geno Auriemma in 1995, he was wearing a sports coat with the lapels turned up like ear muffs and Italian loafers with no socks. It was snowing sideways in Norman, Oklahoma—a typically atypical weather day in the middle of October, which made a gym full of high school athletes as giddy as Geno was confused.

The reigning national championship coach had come to our school, recruiting. I welcomed him and told him to follow us as we drove through the blizzard to our off-site practice facility: an old airplane hanger (where they filmed the movie *Twister*) that we used for practice when the volleyball team was in season in our gym. It was freezing in there. The floor was slick, the lights were lousy, the roof was leaking in a couple of places, and the hottest coach in the world of women's basketball was sitting discreetly on an aluminum bleacher, watching too many girls for one court go through Fast Break in Twos. Oddly enough, he looked perfectly at home.

He told me afterward that I ran a great practice. "You are really good at what you do," he said. Decades later, I can still hear that sentence in my head. What he said mattered because of who he was and what he had done, but how he said it mattered more. He just knew the entry point—kind of like a great nurse who can find the vein on the first try. He gets in and gets you to hear him. I knew then what it must feel like to play for him. You're immediately on his terms. And his terms are in another stratosphere. A place where the cords are cut and the air is impossibly thin, but there is no lid on the sky. Not just anybody can play for Geno Auriemma. It isn't easy and it doesn't always feel good, even though at the beginning you might think it's going to. But he takes you places. And if you really want to go, you find a way to survive.

Several months later, when I readied myself to apply for the head coaching position at the University of Oklahoma, I asked Geno for advice. He told me he was certain that I could do the job; the question was, could I get it? His response was just what the doctor ordered: fuel for my competitive fire and validation for my youth and collegiate coaching inexperience. It left me simultaneously bold and irritated. The man could stick a wooden spoon inside you and stir your soul.

I called him one evening the following fall as my Oklahoma team flipped and flopped while we toiled desperately to build a program. I was overwhelmed, frustrated, and in dire need of a soft place to land. Much to my chagrin, what I got was anything but that. Geno listened as I whined and cried and cited all the things everybody needed me to do for them. And when I finally took a breath, this is what he said: "Do you know what your job is? Your job," he said, "is to be whatever they need for you to be. If that's a teacher, then teach; if it's a cheerleader, then cheer; if it's a counselor, then counsel. That's it.

Period. Do your job." Uhhhhh. Thank you? Stunned, I hung up the phone as quickly as I could. I was shocked, and I think more than a little embarrassed, and I was mad. I specifically remember being mad. And oh so determined to do my job. Ahhh, his magic: the ability to give you what you needed, not so much what you wanted, and to package it in a way that you felt it in the marrow of your bones.

Years later, I served as Geno's assistant for USA Basketball, where I was allowed a peek into his genius as a coach. It was there I discovered it's not all roses being him. He saw the game with seasoned eyes and felt it like a blind man. Lesser levels of understanding created a chaos for him that was almost intolerable. When he couldn't get buy-in from all ports, it pained him in a way most folks can't even feel.

And it doesn't matter what was at stake; it could just as easily be bragging rights at the YMCA as pursuit of a gold medal. With Geno, it was always about how you did it, not what you got for it. Unfortunately, even though he won way, way, way more than he lost, he lived every day as a tortured soul. Because of how he saw the game and all the players in it, he couldn't unsee the gaps between what was and what could be. His genius was at once his blessing and his curse.

In 2002, as witty fate would have it, my Oklahoma Sooners played Geno's Connecticut Huskies for the national title. It couldn't have been more surreal. The whole game is still like slow-drip molasses in my mind. We got them on an offensive counter and I couldn't help but smirk. Then he got us on a flash and back cut, and he gave a toothy grin while clapping and looking directly at me as I fumed. It was the most fun I've ever had in a loss—mainly because competing against him and his team made me and mine better than we ever could have been if we had played a lesser foe.

I don't know that my perspective on the guy is more accurate than anyone else's, but it is certainly unique. He recruited one of my players, I was his assistant coach, and we coached against one another in a national championship game. We've been friends for over thirty years, and I may not know much, but I do know this for sure: as keen as his gift is for x's and o's, Geno's gift for transforming people is greater.

He changes you, if you let him. He twists you up and makes you untie yourself, which is where the education lies. And he thins the air around you while you do it. Gone is room for error; gone is space for praise. That's the secret sauce of how and why he wins. And how he builds the people that do the winning. He strips the air of any unnecessary gunk that might get in the way of success. What remains is an environment where only champions thrive.

WE CAN DO THIS

ONE OF MY MANY TASKS as president of the Women's Basketball Coaches Association (WBCA) was to preside over the yearly coaches' convention held at the NCAA Final Four. Unfortunately, for the coaches whose teams didn't make it, the Final Four is slightly less than fabulous. The pageantry surrounding it serves as a fastidious reminder of your ineptitude. To be president of your coaches' association and not be playing is to sit in the anti-catbird seat. That was my lot that April. Nonetheless, I flew to Tampa, Florida with my upper lip stiff and my game face tightly screwed on. My goal was to take care of business, do my job, and return unscathed. I can still hear Meatloaf singing, "Two Out of Three Ain't Bad."

One of my responsibilities in presiding over our coaches association was to lead our Division I business meeting. This was a little like going to a dentist who doesn't believe in novocaine or happy gas. The business meeting was where coaches had an open forum in which to express their disappointment in the bracketing process, officiating, and any number of other items that they deemed to have cost them at the least their bonus, and at the most their jobs. My role was to guide the discussions without taking sides (think Switzerland in global affairs). This year's "trying to get a word in edgewise" (a.k.a. guiding) only lasted two hours and forty minutes. I kid you not. A member of our fraternity timed it. That's the taking-care-of-business part. I'm proud to announce that despite the torture, we made it safely to the other side.

Another part of my job was to address all of the various entities who met at the convention: high school coaches, junior college coaches, Division II and III coaches, male coaches of women's basketball, black coaches of women's basketball...the president makes the rounds. And here's where I failed to return unscathed. As I went from body to body explaining what the WBCA does—how it can serve, why all coaches are important, how everyone matters—I got drenched in the juju of Kay Yow.

Let me explain. In the fall of 2007, Kay Yow set out to raise significant funds for the fight against all cancers affecting women. This insidious disease attacks one in every seven females. In the coaching profession, that means your neighbor. When you think of a basketball team, that means at least two from every single squad will fight this monster for their lives. When Coach Yow, one of our own, had to rise up to battle for the third time, it was the ultimate teachable moment. Her personal fight became our professional war, and through the indefatigable efforts of the WBCA leadership, ESPN executives, Nike, and Coach Yow herself, within a year's time the Kay Yow/WBCA Cancer Fund was real. A nonprofit helped birth a nonprofit, and money was pouring in from all directions faster than anybody could count it.

Coach Yow is certainly not the first nor the only NCAA Division I head basketball coach to battle cancer, but her fight was undoubtedly the wind beneath our wings. Coach Yow's southern drawl drove the North Carolina (NC) State Wolfpack for over thirty years. She led NC State to twenty of twenty-six NCAA tournaments and was one of only six Division I coaches to win 700 games. Coach Yow was one of those rare competitors whom nobody hates—and that was before she got sick.

Coach Yow not only let the world watch her fight cancer, she invited us to. We were all allowed to witness how she lived with the disease, refusing to bow down to it. She coached bald, wearing the coolest chandelier earrings in town; she coached in a wig, with bandages covering the tips of her fingers where nails used to be; she coached in a white Nike sweatsuit with a big pink ribbon sewn on the chest. She even took chemo on a plane en route to coach an NCAA tournament game. We all admired her fight, so we wore pink shoes and gave away pink shirts and played with pink basketballs, trying to say, "You are not alone out there. A nation of coaches has your back, and we will not go quietly."

Back to the WBCA convention. As I made my way through meeting after meeting at the Final Four, I was in awe of how the countenance of every room shifted when I began to speak about the Pink Zone campaign and the potential impact of the Kay Yow Cancer Fund. It happened every time. Whatever the level, whatever the issues, whatever the size of the group, the Kay Yow cause galvanized the room. I watched the most competitive people on the planet shed their own selfish skins and lock arms for a cause outside themselves, and I was reminded of what it is that makes this thing we do so great.

We fight.

Like rabid, stubborn dogs, we fight. Some of what we fight for and fight over is infantile and purposeless. Sometimes it matters, but it's not important. And then along comes Kay Yow, and the fog lifted. We got permission in an almost spiritual sense to do what we do best. Together. All on the same team.

What our "nation of coaches" was able to do in year one of the creation of a foundation is unheard of. Even the folks at what the world viewed as our "parent nonprofit", the renowned Jimmy V, were stunned. So after a fabulous start, what's the ultimate goal? One summer, over my plate of nachos and her bowl of soup in Augusta, Georgia, Kay made it sound simple: "We raise $5 million in 2009," she said. She had the mathematical formula for doing it down pat in her mind, which she showed me on a napkin in long multiplication form. And she just kept saying, "Can you imagine?"

"Can you imagine if every Division I basketball team gave one hundred dollars? Can you imagine if every high school team gave ten dollars? Can you imagine if every little girl who plays basketball gave one dollar?" Her eyes got bigger and her voice got higher with every exemplification. "Then," she said, almost whispering, as if it were a wonderful secret that she couldn't contain for one second more, "we fund the researcher who finds the cure for breast cancer. And every women's basketball coach in America will be able to be a part of that." As she said that to me, it was painfully clear that THAT was almost as cool to her as finding the cure itself.

One of Kay's favorite stories was about a rural high school near Raleigh, North Carolina, that raised $2,500 at their high school girl's Pack the Place in Pink basketball game in their first attempt at a fundraiser. The young lady who led the charge was a freshman. She told Coach Yow that not only was her team going to raise even more money in the future, but that she was going to train someone to lead the cause once she graduated. The Fund could count on their money from now on.

I loved to hear Coach tell that story because her face just glowed as she talked. I could never quite tell if it was the spunk of the little self-appointed leader that lit her fire, or if it was the concept of exponential expansion: the result of what every little team in America could do collectively to fuel the research for finding a cure for women's cancers.

When Kay Yow talked about the Pink Zone and the development of the next stage of the Fund, you almost forgot the enemy had taken outposts in her blood. Her faith in God, in her doctors, in medicine, in people, and in her profession was profound. As she paused between sips of soup to swallow her newest knight in shining armor—the chemotherapy pill—she seemed almost giddy at the thought of what could be.

"Just one person can make such a difference," she said, her voice dripping in Carolina drawl. "We can do this." And with that thought, my shoulders squared, and I recognized in myself what I had seen repeatedly in coaches at the Final Four. In fighting for Kay and a million other women like her, we played our very best game.

The Kay Yow/WBCA Cancer Fund ultimately became its own 501"c"3 non-profit: the Kay Yow Cancer Fund. At the time of this printing the fund has awarded over $7.88 million for life-saving research and underserved programming. The inaugural Pink Zone game morphed into the nationwide grass roots movement known as Play4Kay. Annual Play4Kay games at every level of girls and women's basketball continue to honor survivors and raise funds for the mission of the Kay Yow Cancer Fund.

A STATELY OAK

ON A FRIDAY AFTERNOON, about the time Rose Hammond ran a back cut to set up a perfect post entry from a position dribble fill, our program lost one of its heroes.

In Ardmore, Oklahoma, on October 26, 2007, Mary Jane Noble slipped quietly from this earth while the program she breathed life into ran around yelping and celebrating subtle excellence in the Oklahoma Sooner manner she so richly enjoyed. We hardly ever quit early. But something about our swagger, something about our joy that day, made me stop our practice short. We were the kind of good you need to think about. I wanted us to stop and go home so we could.

That's when I got the news.

Mary Jane Noble is the name that appears on the side of The University of Oklahoma's Women's Basketball Office Complex. She gave us $8.17 million to build our dream. She said when she wrote the check, "The women's side of the tunnel better not measure one square inch smaller than the men's side when you're finished. I'll be happy to measure it for you when you're through."

Mary Jane was always about right. She was about fair. She was the voice of reason in the midst of panic and high-pitched screams. I always thought she was a woman ahead of her time.

Mary Jane served on the Oklahoma Board of Regents. She was a businesswoman, a philanthropist, a season-ticket holder, and a grandma. She had a way about her that made you simultaneously suck in your stomach and kick off your shoes. The biggest of the bigs sought her counsel. I've never known a woman so admired by decision makers as she was. She was smart and she was stubborn. She was strong. And she was very, very real.

Occasionally, before her health began to decline, Mary Jane would travel with us on charter trips. She nearly always went to Lubbock, Texas with us while her grandson was in school there. He'd come over to the hotel and ride on the bus with us to the gym. She would be in her OU red and he'd have on a Texas Tech Red Raider T-shirt, kindly concealed by a Carhartt jacket. She would gig him about cheering for a losing team and he would grin and take it, knowing that she reveled in the banter as much as she did the game.

My players loved it when she went with us. Our 2002 team adopted her. She went with us to Kansas City, Missouri to the Big 12 Tournament, where my guys couldn't wait to talk to her after the games. She had an uncanny way of putting forty minutes into a sentence in such a manner that hearing about the game was almost as much fun as playing it had been. When we won our first two games in the NCAA tournament and headed for Boise, Idaho and the Sweet 16, our players squealed when they boarded the plane and saw her already on and buckled in. Stacey Dales, our All-American point guard, spent half the trip seated beside her; Stacey, who has gone on to have a tremendous career in broadcast journalism, had a nose for a great interview even then. Dales said to me once, "Coach, Mary Jane Noble is the coolest woman I know." Lots of people felt that way.

Without Mary Jane Noble, Oklahoma Women's Basketball would probably still be flopping around in the trenches of irrelevance. We wouldn't have had the amenities. We wouldn't have had the success. But mostly what we wouldn't have had is a path. Mary Jane walked the walk. The wind could howl and the seas could swirl, but she never wavered. I count her presence among my players a far greater blessing than the gymnasium she built them, but we sorely needed both to become.

There is a tree in north Norman that I love. It stands majestic, by itself, in the middle of a field. A tree line flanks it to the south, but the area immediately around it is barren. No one tends to it. It just stands there alone and thrives. It's as if the brazen oak demands the space it grows in and then some just to be. And it oozes with sureness and serenity and strength. In lots of ways it reminds me of Mary Jane. It asks nothing of you, and you are better just for having driven past it. There's an art to that. I think they call it Presence.

We've been without her now for lots of seasons. I miss the barely legible note cards that followed every big win and the slightly longer letters that followed unexpected losses. But she is with us still. That's the way it works with stately, stubborn oaks and their extraordinary human mimes. You feel them even after they're gone.

"MY HEROES HAVE ALWAYS BEEN COWBOYS"

WHEN I WAS A LITTLE GIRL, I loved the Dallas Cowboys. I had the jersey with stars on the shoulders and the silver helmet with two blue stripes running down the middle. When my brother and I played in the front yard, he always got to be Roger Staubach—number 12. I won't lie; it always irritated me because I thought I threw far better than he did (even though I was four years younger), and I truly expected to grow up and be a quarterback. But mostly, Staubach was just the coolest guy to be. Number 12 jerseys filled the racks in every sock-and-jock store in the country. Staubach was a hero—mine, my brother's, and everyone else's. But I never loved him—not like I loved Bob Lilly, anyway.

Back in the day, the Cowboys had the Doomsday Defense: A line of tough guys with tough names like Jethro Pugh and Chuck Howley and Lee Roy Jordan. They even sounded mean. They had movie-star wide receivers with long blonde hair, a guy they called "Bambi," and a freight train in the backfield named Calvin Hill. There were lots of guys to love. I even had a satin pillowcase with free safety Charlie

Waters's picture on it! But I loved, loved, loved the big, quiet, do-your-job-on-every-play guy anchoring the Doomsday line. Number 74 was my first celebrity crush.

And I have no idea why. I don't recall Bob Lilly being interviewed that much. Don't recall him being on the cover of magazines, except in action photos with grass stains on his uniform and a grimace on his face. But I remember sitting with my dad every Sunday, watching Lilly orchestrate the flow of a football game with a gentleman's ease. I was mesmerized by his way. He'd terrorize quarterbacks, completely eclipsing those he landed on, and then he'd help them off the ground. He was the guy Tom Landry could not say enough good things about—the one who trotted off the field the same way after every defensive stand, whether game altering or not. The big man from the small town just seemed so real, so steady, so tough. And perhaps because he was, he never had to tell you. You just knew.

Over the years, I've been reminded of Bob Lilly a few times. The father of one of our recruits was once his college roommate. I didn't want to ask him many questions, though. The captain of the Doomsday Defense was everything I needed him to be in the pea of my brain already. Too much information can be detrimental to love.

I read a magazine story about Mr. Cowboy a few years ago. When his body wore down and he'd done what he wanted to do on the field, he retired from professional football and followed a passion for photography. Apparently he attacked that venture like he did quarterbacks scrambling in the backfield, and thus became extraordinary. He even published a book of landscape photography. Now he lives in Texas near his three kids and fourteen grandkids.

He doesn't even sound like he's real. But he is.

Quiet greatness. Balance. Superb personal sense of expectation— Bob Lilly is the poster child. And we're tempted, as we reminisce— those of us who even remember Tom Landry's Cowboys—to long wistfully for the good old days. But I don't think they're gone. Substance still exists in professional sports, it's just often in the crevices between all the glitz and clamoring. The steady do-your-job guys are still around. The guys who glue teams together still do their maven work. The ballplayers who passionately pursue excellence because they believe in their game and the type of people it makes them still play. Did you see Jason Witten's retirement press conference? Have you taken a look at Drew Brees's life?

Several years back, I had the remarkable opportunity to meet Roger Staubach at an awards dinner. I introduced myself (trembling, I might add), and he said, "I love your team."

I said, "Excuse me? You watch women's college basketball?"

And he said, "I love it! I love how your team shares the ball; I love how hard they compete. I just think it's great. You know, I have a gym at my house. I play hoops every day. When you're in Dallas, call me. You're welcome anytime."

"Wow! I'm honored," I stuttered. "Any chance Bob Lilly could come?"

MINE WAS BORN LUCKY

ONE SPRING DAY, when I was driving my fifteen-year-old daughter, Chandler, to school and we were calendar meshing for the week ahead, she saw "Title IX Celebration" on my phone and asked what in the world it meant. I jumped on the teachable moment and explained it. "It's the anniversary of the law passed in 1972 that says you get to play basketball like your brother. It's the law that says girls can go to college and study to be anything they want, just like boys can," I added.

To which Chandler responded with a snarled lip and slanted eye, "That's the dumbest thing I've ever heard. Why would anybody need a law to tell them that?"

A new paradigm had been constructed. I had goosebumps from my head to the tip of my toes.

As coaching careers go, mine was born lucky. When I got the job as head coach at the University of Oklahoma, women's basketball was poised for a coming-out party nationwide. New programs and personalities were on the scene, attendance was rising, television was flirting, lightning was begging to be captured in a bottle. I was new to the collegiate scene, barely cognizant of the perfect storm I had landed in the middle of—and yet there I sat at the table with the giants of our game.

I was young and dumb in 1996, but smart enough to be quiet (read: keep opinionated mouth shut) and pay attention. Pioneers in their prime were running the room. Marsha Sharp, as the head coach at Texas Tech, was the captain of the juggernaut known as Lady Raider Nation. She coached Sheryl Swoopes, and together with their throng of faithful followers, they won a National Championship and took west Texas and the country by storm. Jody Conradt sat at the table—a national title, an undefeated season, the architect of Texas women's basketball, and a figure so respected and at times so imposing—that she could have run for governor of that enormous state and won. Across from her sat Ceal Barry, the Colorado coach whose teams won four Big Eight titles and whose tenacious man-to-man defense and post-player development had been building blocks of my philosophy as a high school coach for years. I loved watching her win and I so admired how her teams did it.

Talk about being in the right place at the right time! At those early Big 12 conference meetings where we made decisions about rules, recruiting, scheduling, and TV deals, the topics were dense and the conversations layered. With the grandeur of the Colorado Rocky Mountains in the backdrop, it was often hard to tell if my shortness of breath came from the altitude or the luck of my draw for getting to be a mouse inside that room.

I'm not sure I really knew it at the time, but the twelve of us around that table were readying our sport for a rocket-ship ride.

The room pulsated with that anxious weighty vibe that often hangs around tethered dreams. I could feel it, but I couldn't ever give it a name. I didn't know enough about where we had been to be able to identify where we were, much less where we might be headed, but I knew something way more important than Big 12 business was taking place. I could feel the ragged cusp of it. Every discussion we dove into bore tentacles rooted in a passionate, sacrificial past. From the days of fighting for opportunity to participate, to the lonely plodding of Title IX adjudication once the law was put into place, these women bore the scars of the road less traveled. It was as if they'd been crawling through a tunnel and could finally see a light at the end signaling room to run. Platforms were being built, multi-media contracts were being designed, salaries were set to explode. These women with their eyes locked in on conference minutiae were also crafting a game plan to take women's basketball to the moon.

We were on a mission. That was always crystal clear.

These seasoned coaches were caretakers of the game, first and foremost. They made decisions based on the blood, sweat, and tears of lives spent creating opportunities for women to compete in sports. Discussions about anything and everything as it pertained to the Big 12 conference were always subjected to the litmus test of what is best for our game. It wasn't ever "What is best for Texas, or Colorado, or Texas Tech?" It was always "What is best for women's basketball?" I learned quickly that the sieve through which you pour all issues, great and small, is the one that grows our game. Because that's how you think when pieces of your soul are woven into a thing.

That's the part my generation—those of us who were handed the golden baton—have a hard time understanding. And it is our greatest charge.

Those of us who waltzed into the basketball explosion of the 90s and have been stepping through the doorway ever since don't really know much about life before Title IX. We know about the law; they made us read about it in school. And we get it. But we don't get it like the group I sat with around that table did. And the generation that follows us? They get it even less. Unfortunately, sometimes that's how history works: If we're not careful, if we don't strive to stay connected to it, we can wind up back where we started. We have to remember where we were in order to keep going where we need to go. And I don't know anybody who wants to climb that mountain all over again.

My daughter's generation can't even fathom a world in which girls are not allowed opportunities of participation. She can't comprehend not being able to play ball or go to medical school if she so desires, much the way my generation can't imagine that people actually spat upon Jackie Robinson. That discrimination seems foreign to us. My daughter's generation sees the world through a different lens.

And yet, Chandler and her contemporaries all need to know. We have to tell them the stories, just the way we tell them about Rosa Parks and Martin Luther King, Jr. and Prentice Gautt. We have to tell them about Bernice Sandler, Patsy Mink, and Billie Jean King versus Bobby Riggs. They have to know how they got here so they can understand the responsibilities they hold.

Our charge as stakeholders of our game is to go about our business in the same way that those who gave us the opportunity to be here did. Our challenge is to work with their dogged determination, to compete with their hunger, and to revel in competition with their joy.

Uh oh. That means we can't be entitled brats. We can't coach or play or market or promote apathetically. (I think I just created an oxymoron). We can't whine or mumble or gripe or complain. We have no right, ironically, to play without joy. We disrespect those upon whose shoulders we stand when we do. Our mission is to honor their path with how we do our jobs.

Our mission is to play well.

THE BIG-TIME
SMALL-COLLEGE COACH

I WAS IN THE VERY CENTER OF my happy place when I saw him. He was sitting about two-thirds of the way up the bleachers. I was teaching on court at a Coaches' Clinic, and he was in the audience, sandwiched between a bunch of random guys wearing branded pullovers and balancing Nike notebooks on their knees. His trademark crooked ball cap was sitting awkwardly on his bald head. Don Meyer stood out in a crowd even when he was sitting.

When I spotted him, I lost my breath and my train of thought jumped a track. Not because he was famous, but because at the moment I saw him, what I was talking about was him.

Don Meyer was a giant in my basketball world. He had been a champion at Lipscomb University in Nashville, Tennessee, in the early 80s. He won over 900 games in his career and had a reputation as a guy who excelled at teaching post play, molding character, and being a little odd in the most magical kind of way. I had studied him hard. His quippy phrases and his resolute organization were magnetic to me. I referenced him all the time when I taught. So bringing him up that day at the Nike Clinic where I was teaching wasn't strange, except that he was sitting in the gym when I did it. Hence the thought train that lay mangled in the ditch.

At the time of the sighting, I had my demonstrators from a local small-college men's team sitting in a circle at center court. They were make-believe stretching, and I was talking about what coaches could learn and set in motion for their teams during practice from that circle at the start. I have no idea where that lecture went after I saw Coach Meyer taking notes. His cock-eyed expression is burned in my brain, but everything else gets muddy from that moment on.

After I finished the clinic, I was meeting coaches, taking pictures, and talking ball when I heard someone say, "Is your boyfriend's sweatshirt the only thing Oklahoma will give you to wear?" To which I wheeled around and responded, "Nike doesn't make the cool stuff in a small." And that's when I met Don Meyer.

He was bigger than I imagined, his handshake even more firm. He said something complimentary about the clinic, moving between deadpan cuts and heartfelt flattery in a way that made me dizzy. I liked him immediately, though I'd loved him from afar for a while. So when he asked if he could ask me a question, I was nothing if not all ears.

Coach asked me to come speak at his Academy. He was coaching at Northern State in Aberdeen, South Dakota, and had built a coaches' workshop that gym rats with whistles around their necks stood in line to get into. He wanted me to come teach—to headline his event. He said Pat Summit had come up and done it one year, and that last year, John Wooden was the guy. I'm pretty sure I quit breathing when he name-dropped the Wizard of Westwood. I felt like I was in the rafters watching somebody else's life.

So of course, I agreed. It couldn't be next summer soon enough.

When it came time to fly to Aberdeen, I discovered that it wasn't any closer to Oklahoma than I thought it was, and it was a lot harder to get to than I'd imagined. Coach said there'd be somebody at the airport to pick me up and bring me straight to the gym, and that I wouldn't need a hotel room. I'd just stay at his place. His wife, Carmen, welcomed all, and wouldn't have it any other way. I was a tad outside my comfort zone but convinced I'd fallen headfirst into every coach's dream.

A guy did pick me up at the airport. I think he was a graduate assistant (Coach always had a few, whether they were really in school or not). And he was of typical Don Meyer lineage. He met me at the curb with a broad smile—and a well-worn Plymouth that had a hole in the passenger side floor. I did my best to play it cool, as if I saw this all the time, trying to cover it nonchalantly with my foot as we lurched our way toward the gym. On the drive, we talked hoops and clinic attendance expectations and what this young man hoped to do when the dirty work of summer camps in Aberdeen was done. Then, in vintage small-college form, he dropped me off at the door to the Physical Education building, like an Uber driver before that was even a thing. I couldn't help but chuckle under my breath as I tried a series of locked doors, trying to find one that would let me in. Everything about the pick up and delivery screamed Don Meyer. I could not believe my luck.

After finding my own way to Coach's office—a tiny space where papers were stacked taller than the oversized people crammed in the room—I stuffed my bags in the only empty corner I could find and tried to stay out of the way as organized mayhem played out around me. I was ready to teach and excited to do so, but more than anything, I had come to Aberdeen to learn. The education started before we ever got to the court. Coach eventually took me to the gym, where I did my deal while the coaches took notes voraciously. When I finished, I joined them in the stands, filling up my own legal pad while others shared the game. It was the most fun I'd ever had for free.

As promised, I stayed at Coach's house—me and what felt like thirty other coaches. People seemed to just keep coming through the doors, and though I wasn't sure how everyone was going to fit, I wasn't the least bit surprised. Great coaches create tribes who continually descend and congregate no matter where life takes them. The Meyer tribe was as loud and loyal as they come, and they sought out the Academy as a time and place to reconvene. I perched on the kitchen counter and took every last bit of it in.

As the years went by, this small college phenom grew more and more famous, renowned beyond his region or his level or the circles where his teaching was ingrained. His aphorisms took on a life of their own with the assistance of the internet, as people everywhere could suddenly share the truths Don Meyer espoused.

Coach's life has been well documented since his death. As the result of a catastrophic car crash, the doctors discovered cancer he didn't know he had. He spent the last four years of his life pushing his physical limits while traveling the world, teaching, and sharing all the wisdom he had mined throughout his days. He gave until his body had no more to give, and he spent a lot of those last days making the rounds, checking on his guys.

He even stopped by my gym on a Sunday afternoon. Our team took a picture with him, and he signed it. I hope my girls remember some of what he said. Even if they don't, I know they felt him there. That was nonnegotiable; he penetrated any skin.

I think about Don Meyer's life a lot. He loved Jesus. He loved his family. He loved his guys. His life was an arc expressing the 'thoroughly used up when I die' kind of life that George Bernard Shaw wrote about. Coach Meyer wasn't perfect—Carmen and his kids can tell you about the rough spots—but he did so much good. His path was a long and winding road, and so many lives are better for having crossed it. I'm honored to count mine among them.

TROUBLE

ONE EVENING, I dragged my nineteen-year-old daughter, Chandler, to a tiny Oklahoma City music venue called The Blue Door. The jaunt was a bit outside of our beaten path, but a friend had called and asked us to go to hear an under-the-radar talent whom she knew I had heard and loved. I had too much to do to go and my daughter had nothing better, so we met there anyway at the vibey little joint named for the way you don't go in.

Liz Longley made us both so glad we did.

Liz Longley is a singer-songwriter whose voice is like a slip-and-slide for angels. She travels the country in a minivan with guitars, a keyboard, some amps and speakers, and a dog she adores. Before that night at the Blue Door, I'd only ever heard two or three of her songs, but I loved what I knew. Her lyrics were distinctly honest and her chords uniquely paired. Listening live to the journey of her life through her setlist was similar to being in an escape room: her lyrics are like clues that take you by the hand and walk you through the twisted insides of yourself.

That random night in front of sixty or so eclectic music lovers, Liz played funny stuff and break-up stuff and feel-good stuff and think-hard stuff. And when she played "Unraveling," my daughter and I did.

"Unraveling" is a haunting song about losing a loved one, one memory at a time. This was the first time my daughter had heard the song. It was one of the three I knew. I had run across it while Dad was sick, still in the throes of his lengthy heavyweight bout with the disease Liz wrote and sang about; the disease that siphons its victims' minds, and in so doing, the blood from the hearts of everybody who loves them. "Unraveling" was on my playlist, but I'd hit 'next' every time it came around. It was just too raw and too foreboding for me at that time.

It hit my grown-up baby girl that way on Monday night. Hard and unsuspecting, right between the eyes.

Two rows away from the guitar and the voice, Chan ducked her head and cried buckets under the tent of her long blonde hair. My wounds, too, were still gaping, but they felt less wet. In the midst of that tiny intimate group of strangers, I found "Unraveling" to be oddly soothing—the words, Liz's voice, the memories. I felt weirdly wrapped up in a blanket by the commonness of pain.

And in the exposure of that space, inside the little place they call the Blue Door, I discovered that grief sits in containers and sometimes the lids pop off of one, spilling the contents of another.

Several years ago, God crossed my path with a feisty little girl named Mackenzie. She was at war with cancer, and I was on my monthly quest for relevance outside of the bubble of college athletics. Children's Hospital reminds you how big the picture really is. Angels abound there always, and every once in a while one throws a lasso around your heart.

Kenzie roped mine.

We shared lots of moments, Kenzie and I—some in the cubicles at Children's, some in the radiation waiting room, some in my office at the gym, a few at her favorite places to eat. She was inspiration on wheels. This precious woman-child, who packed more life in her brief candle than most humans do in ninety years, died one week after her thirteenth birthday. When she did, she took pieces of a lot of hearts with her. She certainly took a chunk of mine.

The in-between part of the story is what pertains to Liz and the Blue Door.

One day, as Kenzie and I sat in the infusion lab one-upping one another with obscure songs from our smartphones, I played Liz Longley's "When You've Got Trouble," a song that wraps its melody around you like the metaphorical vine that is its hook. Kenzie downloaded it right away. A few weeks later, she texted me a video of her playing it on her guitar. Her voice was soft and sincere. She seemed three times her age.

"Trouble" (as we called it) grew to be our anthem. It lifted her—made her feel strong and vulnerable at the same time. And it said everything my brain was thinking but felt too much to say. We played it when I lost games and she got bad reports. Somehow in those patches of respective rough water, "Trouble" kept her from drowning and me from swimming away.

Kenzie was a warrior princess in a body ravaged by cancer with a capital C. I always felt like she must be having side conversations with God that the rest of us weren't capable of, because she just got things before and better than everybody else did. She loved like Jesus, and maybe better than anyone I have ever known. Even the cancer couldn't make her hate.

And as much as that little girl believed in Heaven, she fought desperately not to go—not yet anyway. I felt her valiant spirit all around me as she slowly, physically wasted away. I feel it still, usually just when I need it most.

That night at The Blue Door, Liz Longley sang about shared troubles and the entanglement of souls trying to make the way better for each other.

And it all washed over me. Kenzie's courage. Dad's perseverance. The resolution to bow to grace in the face of the bad and ugly when we do not have the power to amend it. The blessing of having both of those amazing humans in my life. It all got tangled up inside the notes wafting through that Oklahoma dive, at a free concert in the place where the door you enter is everyday brown.

PART IV

Diverse Inhabitants

"Redwood trees are home to amphibians, beetles, crickets, worms, millipedes, spiders and mollusks. The clouded salamander, a species that breathes entirely through its skin and has a prehensile tail for climbing, thrives in the canopy. Chipmunks, fishers, peregrine falcons, bald eagles, the northern spotted owl, the marbled murrelet, and dozens of other species call the canopy home. California condors were found nesting in the cavities of giant sequoias, and these evergreen behemoths are home to at least six species of bat. The redwood forest creates not only a unique ecosystem on the ground, but also across every inch of space hundreds of feet above the soil. Researchers are still learning about the deeply intricate lives of redwoods."

–Jaymi Heinbuck, Treehuger

"*The tree is more than first a seed,*

then a stem, then a living trunk,

and then dead timber.

The tree is a slow, enduring force

straining to win the sky."

—ANTOINE DE SAINT-EXUPÉRY

THE FOUNDATION

A FRIEND OF A FRIEND of my college coach is how I found Phylesha Whaley. She was from Slaton, Texas, a little town west of Lubbock where the tumbleweeds roll and very little stands to eclipse the view—or would if there was a view anybody ever wanted to see. Phylesha had grown up a Texas Tech Lady Raider basketball fan. And rightly so. Hall of Fame Coach Marsha Sharp had built an amazing program in a women's basketball hotbed where thousands of little dribblers on the plains and beyond shared Phylesha's dream. Basketball teams, however, can only have fifteen players. In the spring of 1996, Phylesha failed to make the cut.

Around the same time her dream was crumbling, mine at Oklahoma was taking root. I'd just been named the head coach, and I needed players. Immediately, if not sooner. Not many game-changing players are left hanging around in April, but we were bound and determined to dig. Stephanie Findley, my own college coach, was on my volunteer gold-mining team. She's the one who panned the lucrative streams of West Texas high schools where we discovered Phylesha Whaley, the one gold nugget no one had yet found.

Signing date was rapidly approaching and the official visit window was closing with it, so I called Chris Kennedy, the Slaton High School coach, and began the recruiting process in fast forward. On the wings of an introductory phone call, we invited Phylesha to come to campus for the weekend. In the meantime, I waited for some game film to show me what she could do.

Phylesha and her mom, Cynara, flew in from Texas. We showed them our campus, our arena, the city of Norman, and purposefully not our dorms. We took them to dinner, introduced them to our team, and sat eyeball to eyeball for an hour, just talking about our dreams. This wide-eyed kid left a trail of sincerity everywhere she went, but I still had absolutely no idea what she could do with a ball in her hand.

I checked the mail and called the coach as the NCAA-mandated forty-eight-hour official visit evaporated without me having ever seen her play. She was precious. She was respectful and kind and interested and hungry to be great. But I couldn't offer her a scholarship sight unseen! I was a rookie coach who had no idea what I was doing and little to no evidence with which to formulate a logical decision.

I was as transparent as glass, telling her I'd call her as soon as I had a chance to watch her game tape, but I couldn't offer her a scholarship yet. Not yet. I had to be sure. Phylesha and her mom were amazing. We took them to the airport. As we waited for her flight, I happened into the restroom and overheard Phylesha praying in the stall. Every atom in my body wanted to offer her a scholarship right there on the spot. But I didn't. This decision could be a part soul call, but that couldn't be the all of it. This was an important decision—for her and me I had to do it right.

The following Tuesday, Phylesha's film arrived. I must have watched it forty times.

Her team had lost in overtime in the class 3A Texas State Championship. She scored thirty-three points and had thirteen rebounds. And she was a 5' 10" high school player who played at the low block with her back to the basket. She made lay-ups and free throws. Slaton got a lot of both. She never shot it from the perimeter, she didn't appear to be fast, and she never got to dribble. I had everyone I knew watch that tape. The response was always the same: shrugged shoulders and open palms. She was a good high school player whose film projected little guarantee of next-level success. There was just no way to know.

But there was something about her eyes.

As I wrestled with the decision at hand, I just kept thinking, "My first signee as a Division I basketball coach is going to be a 5' 10" center." As every roster on the planet had at least two players over 6' 4", how in the world could we compete if she was the anchor of our inside game? The left side of my brain was saying, "There's a reason it is April and she has nowhere to play," while the right side of my brain was saying, "This kid is not typical; she has a spirit you can feel." The battle waged inside my head: fact versus feeling. Oh, how I wanted a formula for figuring it out.

Finally, I closed my eyes and jumped. I offered Phylesha Whaley a scholarship to attend the University of Oklahoma. She screamed and accepted on the spot. There was a lot of laughing and celebrating and gratitude-sharing across the phone line. There was weeping and promising and planning, too.

There was just something about her eyes.

In 1996, our program needed a lot of things. We needed size. We needed speed. We needed a shooter. But maybe more than anything, we needed somebody who was willing to run through a wall. A player who could set her jaw and would. Somebody tough enough to endure the losing—because there was going to be some—and yet smart enough to know in her bones that it wouldn't be for long. In short, we needed true believers. We needed someone to model what I was teaching, someone with broad enough shoulders to carry the expectations and sticky enough hands to keep people with her. This was not a job for a scaredy cat. Thank goodness Phylesha Whaley was anything but that.

As promised, our first two years were rough. We won five games in the first, three more than that in the second—yet the private victories were preceding the public ones at record speed.

In the middle of it all, Phylesha Whaley was becoming a household name in Oklahoma. All those inside of and around our program just referred to her as P-Dub.

P-Dub was our leading scorer. She was also our leading rebounder. She was also the player we went to when we had to have a basket or the game was on the line. She played more minutes than anyone. I called timeouts when she got tired.

People couldn't guard her. I would have commiserated with them had we not been getting our brains beat in, because she was a handful. I didn't know what I would do if charged with trying to keep her from scoring points. She had developed the ability to shoot three-pointers and she was money from the high post. She still got fouled a ton, and you could bet the house on her point-blank putbacks—she just never missed close range. And on top of all that, she had this uncanny ability to create space. She used a bevy of tools: a stabbing shot fake, a whipping reverse pivot dribble, a now-you-see-it-now-you-don't up-and-under move, and a hook shot you could never predict when she was going to release.

She could do it all. That's how she became P-Dub. Just like Elvis and Oprah, nobody else could do what she did.

But the best part was always who she was.

P-Dub said "thank you" to the managers when they handed her a bottle of water during a heated game. She handed the ball to the refs. She pointed to the person who passed her the ball when she scored, and she gave God the credit after every single game. I fell in love with her eyes and signed her because of what I saw there, but I'd be lying if I said I knew this was what we were getting when she came.

In the fall of her junior year, we began a random afternoon practice with a thirty-five-second line drill (typically reserved for punishment) for no apparent reason. I lined them up and blew the whistle; P-Dub won it, as she usually did. She was confused, but always compliant. With her hands on her hips, elbows fanned to the side, she fidgeted on the baseline, visually checking her teammates for cracks. You could have heard a pin drop in our gym.

"Being in the top twenty-five doesn't mean anything," I said. "Don't get fat and sassy just because we're there."

P-Dub connected the dots and screamed, and our team went ballistic. There was crying and shouting and a dogpile on the court. She was teaching even then: this is how you celebrate the steps... this is how you feel the payoff... this is how much fun it is to do what others say can't be done. She was the living, breathing example of substance. Her teammates loved her in places inside of themselves they couldn't even find.

When Phylesha was a senior, we won the conference title. We also got to go mad in March with sixty-three other teams. P-Dub gladly pulled the wagon we all jumped in, as she led us to a new frontier. While our draw was less than awesome, no one in our camp seemed to notice. We had been saying for nine months that we would be playing in the Sweet 16 in March, and we were two wins away from that goal. Details like where and when and who were for other people to worry about. We had more important stuff to do.

Our regional site was West Lafayette, Indiana, which meant we were going to Purdue University to play on the home floor of the defending national champions. The difficulty inherent in that never crossed our determined minds.

Rolling into town, we took pictures of everything: the billboard that advertised the Final Four, the signs that flanked the front of the arena, the hotel and its welcome. We were the quintessential tourists on a dreamscape in the middle of Nowhere, USA.

After a shaky start by both teams in the beginning of round one, we forged ahead and won decidedly. Round two would be against Purdue. They were bigger than us and individually more talented, and they were certainly more accustomed to the stage. All of that was evident by halftime. We struggled to score and had no answers for their half-court offense. We made an iffy basket before the buzzer at halftime that took us to the locker room trailing Purdue by twelve, but it never felt that close.

Our team was so authentic, so honest about who they were and what they wanted, it was always easy to tell them what they needed to know. So at halftime, I did. I told them we had had a remarkable year. I told them twenty minutes was a long time left to play, but it wouldn't last forever, so it was really only appropriate for us to do one thing.

Play for P-Dub.

Run, jump, smile, hug, and revel in the time that you are guaranteed on the court with this once-in-a-lifetime leader. "Wring it dry," I said. "Whatever happens, happens. But we can live out loud doing what we love for the next twenty minutes in an attempt to honor her."

"Love her," I told our warriors. "Love her with how you play."

At the first media timeout of the second half, we were down fourteen. My halftime rah-rah was so good it had us going the wrong way! But by the next timeout, we had cut it to eleven. At the next one, we had it down to eight. All of a sudden, it was game on. As the clock ticked down, we had the ball, down by one, and I called a timeout to set up a play that we ran to perfection.

Unfortunately, Purdue guarded it that way, too.

What happened next is why you teach, and it's also why players, not coaches, win games. Stacey Dales, our future All-American point guard, took the busted play and centered the ball on a dribble. LaNeishea Caufield, her cool-as-a-cucumber backcourt buddy, ran a fist and back cut from the right wing to the block. Dales laid down a textbook bounce pass that Caufield fielded and tried to finish through a punishing foul. The ball didn't go in, but she made the two free throws, and we had our first lead. With 1:03 on the clock, we were up by one.

The final minute was a hold-your-breath blur. We did everything we could to keep from fouling. They chased us and tackled us to send us to the free throw line. Dales made a couple, missed one, and with only seconds left to play, we were up three and there was nothing Purdue could do.

The upset was history.

Six thousand people sat stunned in tomb-like silence while all twenty-five of us—team and travel party—lost our collective minds. ESPN cut to our ending for the "stunner in West Lafayette," as Beth Mowins proclaimed. The world got to see the program P-Dub built. Beth asked P-Dub courtside how on earth such a thing could be.

"How does a team who's never been to the NCAA tournament come from a double-digit deficit at halftime to beat the defending national champions on their home floor?" she asked.

To which P-Dub responded, "It's what we said we were going to do. Every day. All year long." Her big, brown eyes packed the heat behind the words.

On senior night, our players all wore T-shirts with Phylesha's picture on the front and all her records and accomplishments listed around it. The back said, "Thank you, P-Dub." She was our only senior that year. I always found that fitting. If there had been others, they would have burned up in her light.

My first big decision as a major league basketball coach turned out to be a dandy. I don't know that I coached a more impactful player in my entire career. Phylesha was what you hoped the arrow stopped on when spinning the big wheel on *The Price is Right*. Outwardly, she appeared so average; her physical packaging camouflaged almost everything that was giant inside her.

Fortunately, however, it could not hide her eyes.

THE PINK LADDER

I BOUGHT A PINK LADDER. It happened fast in a bidding war at a Kay Yow Cancer Fund event, but it was for a great cause, so I didn't mind writing the check at all. I have to admit, however, that I had no idea what I was going to do with a really expensive ladder, especially a pink one. So when it arrived on my doorstep, I called my equipment manager to bring a truck out to my house and ferry it to our gym. A few borderless ideas were already forming in my head; I would find a way to use it. We'd make it matter. I just wasn't quite sure how.

A couple of weeks later, I met with my team on a Wednesday.

We were in our film room. A stack of stats sat in front of me, a teaching edit was waiting to be played on the projector, and a pink ladder stood awkwardly in the front corner of the room. The 2012 season was in the books, and my tremendous group of warriors, still a bit gaunt and more than a wee bit agitated about the premature ending of their season, were strung out across the room.

On that seemingly innocuous Wednesday, we talked about all the things you talk about when a season ends. And then we talked about all the things you talk about when you prepare for another—one you'd like to see finished with trophies, confetti, and pieces of net that you cut from a championship goal. Then I introduced them to the elephant in the room.

I told them the brief, abridged version of how that ladder got to Norman, Oklahoma, and then I told them how special it was going to be for our team. We talked about the Kay Yow Cancer Fund. We talked about Coach Yow and her courageous battle with this insidious disease. We talked about the power of our platform as a collegiate team of women, and we talked about the symbolism of a ladder in our gym all off-season: the daily reminder it could be to us of where we wanted to go and what it would take to get there.

Then I launched my plan for our pink ladder.

I introduced our team to the concept of six-word memoirs: life statements power-packed into only six words, usually simple ones strung together in formidable ways. (Think Twitter as a euphemistic Shrinky Dink). There is a website; I had a book. We looked at examples—some created raucous laughter, others brought tears. Then I asked our team to come up with their own six-word memoirs that reflected their lives as athletes. "What six words would summarize your journey?" I asked.

I gave them one week to come up with their own six words and tattoo them onto the pink ladder in Sharpie marker. Their individual memoirs would be territorial marks on the symbolic tool that would stand in our gym over the summer months. It would be a tangible reminder that would constantly spur us on.

You could almost see the wheels racing in their heads. This group "got it." They would run with this idea, I could tell. And I could not wait to see what next Wednesday held.

Then two days later, on Friday, life threw us a daunting curve. The biopsy came back positive, and the ladder took on a life of its own.

My assistant for sixteen years, my college teammate, the maid of honor at my wedding, and our team's rudder, Jan Ross, was diagnosed with breast cancer. It was the call you never want to get. The words you never want to hear. Reality morphed immediately into a slow-motion slosh through phone calls and emails and to-do lists that helped the two of us feel like we were somehow in charge of it all, though deep down inside we knew we were running in place.

Telling the team was the worst, I think. For those who had nursed loved ones through their own heavyweight fights with cancer, the response was courageous defiance. We could all put a face and a name on what was about to happen—the journey had a form for us. But for those who had never been down such a path, the terror was mysterious and raw. We prayed together. Whitney Hand, our team captain, led her peers with the wisdom and the strength of a woman twice her age. And the days dragged on.

Pink Ladder due date, May 2, came and went. Jan and I were otherwise engaged. We set the surgery date, met with each member of the cancer fight team, and did the hurry-up-and-wait deal like we were professionals. Then one afternoon, during an itchy spell when we'd checked off all the items on our respective lists, I thought about the ladder and asked if she'd like to go down to see it. I secretly wondered if our players had even remembered what I'd asked them to do, much less gotten around to doing it. In the fog of the last few days, it would have been an easy assignment to forget. And no one would have blamed the players for the whiff.

Except they didn't. Whiff, that is. Our guys hit that curveball smoothly out of the park.

Their six-word memoirs graced the legs of the ladder, each neatly printed in individual fonts. I could almost see the ghosts of their personal gravitas as they traced them there. It's really not an exercise you can do lightly. Then in the middle of trying to match the memoir with the athlete, we saw it: six words, each written elegantly, yet with an "I mean it" bravado, on its own rung. Our team's mission for the year ahead: "Playing for our Rock, Coach Ross."

Precious, priceless moment.

That pink ladder mattered. And though I sure didn't see it coming, now I know exactly how.

SPREADER OF JOY

I THINK I MIGHT ALWAYS feel the heaving sobs of Whitney Hand in my arms when it was finally all over. Hers had been a storied career. But it was the anti-fairytale, the real life, living-color story of the folk fable *A Tale of Three Trees*. We always seem to get what we want, just not in the ways we had imagined. Every uphill climb of her collegiate basketball journey seemed to birth yet another bend in the road, and when her final page turned, the depth of her heart-and-soul investment spilled out like volcanic ash.

It was awful. It was magical. It is imprinted in my bones. And she and it are exactly why I did what I did for more than a quarter of a century. That much I know for sure.

Whit walked onto the University of Oklahoma campus in the summer of 2008, joining a stellar cast of athletes who had been heralded as the crew that would take us to the moon, but hadn't yet and was running out of time. She bounced in, led by an irresistible smile and trailed by a long, braided ponytail. She ran on her tip-toes, hugged with all her muscles, and cried at the drop of a hat. Her heart was bigger than a house. None of us could have known then, though, how the next five years would require her to live in every room of it. Her career at Oklahoma would eventually force her to explore every nook and cranny while spending lots of time in the places she'd rather never go.

As a freshman, Whit immediately established herself as our hardest worker. We knew what we would get from her every single day. And she infused us with joy. Playing ball was Whitney's passion. It wasn't what she did; it was what she lived to do. She could change the countenance of a gym by running onto the floor. I always challenged our teams to play in such a way that people walking to their cars when the game was over would say to themselves, "I want to be a better me." When Whitney played, they did.

Early in her freshman year, Whit caught the world by storm. As a coach, you hope for all your athletes that they get that day—that forty-minute span when the stars align perfectly and the world is theirs for the taking. Whit's came quickly, and it showed up on the grandest of stages, a game played in primetime on ESPN.

On February 2, 2009, on ESPN's Big Monday, we faced Tennessee for a non-conference matchup, a contractual game that had been scheduled a couple of years before, but had now become a marquee pairing thanks to the success of both our seasons. As fate would have it, the Lady Vols came to town carrying with them Pat Summitt's 999 wins. The iconic coach was one win away from becoming the winningest NCAA basketball coach of all time. And the throngs clamoring for 1,000 came with her. The game was to be played in Oklahoma City at the NBA arena anyway, but it turned out to be a necessary forum for the circus and all its props. The nationally televised game quickly morphed into an *event* in which we were simply pawns. All eyes in the world of women's basketball—and even in the sports world and beyond—were on our game, but not on us.

The Tennessee program requested a rack of sixteen game balls to be changed out at every media timeout so that the 1,000th win might be authenticated with Pat's autograph following the landmark win. (For the record, we didn't oblige.) They asked for multiple Gatorade containers for housing confetti that would be tossed as the crowning final buzzer blew. Media descended from everywhere and Hall of Famer Bob Knight came to town to call the game. Lucky Oklahoma—we were going to get to be a part of the show.

Some 16,000 people jammed into the OKC arena to watch history. Most were proudly wearing their crimson and cream flags, though a solid section glowed with Tennessee orange. And then there was a sea of folks who weren't even women's basketball fans—just people who wanted to be able to say they were there when it happened.

Except that they weren't. Because it didn't. Not on that night in our town.

What was supposed to be Pat's night turned into Whitney's show. After falling behind early, we roared back on a series of back-door cuts and a couple of transition three-pointers. By halftime, we had folks a little nervous, as Bobby Knight was all about our spacing and timing and the heady play of our little point guard who was making things happen with her speed. Contributions were coming from everywhere. And play by play, whether she was the one scoring or not, Whitney's smile just kept getting broader. As we ran off the floor at intermission, it was clear that the bipartisan crowd had gotten swept up in her joy.

By the end of the game, Coach Knight was taken by our team, but he had fallen head over heels in love with Whitney Hand. If words can sound like drool, his did—and rightly so. Her stat line that night read eight of nine from the field, four of five from three-point land, twenty points, two rebounds, two steals, one block, and forty minutes played. She had been at her best when her best was required, and she'd done it in movie-star style.

Final score: Oklahoma 80, Tennessee 70. Pat's confetti would have to wait.

That night was extraordinary on a million and one levels, but mostly it reigned perfect because the world got a glimpse of our girl.

That season, in her inaugural campaign, Whit led us to the Final Four. Despite missing four games late in the year with a broken finger, she returned for postseason play and quickly re-established herself as the axis around which we turned. After winning two games at home, we made the trek up I-35 to Oklahoma City for the Midwest Regional, where we rolled over a talented Pittsburg team in the NCAA round of Sweet 16. Then in the Regional Championship—the game that propels you to the Final Four—Whit's tenacious way took over.

We went back and forth for twenty-eight minutes with Purdue. At the 10:26 mark of the second half, after going to the low block for baskets—a strategy they had to make concessions to thwart—on two consecutive possessions, we called the counter to our post-feed play: a three for Whit off an elevator screen.

She nailed it. And we never trailed again.

That night, Whit went three of twelve from the field and three of eight from behind the arc. She only scored nine points in thirty-nine minutes of toil, but we could not *not* have her on the floor. She was that kid who made everyone around her better just by being there. We wouldn't have won that game without her. If she hadn't been there, there would have been no 2009 Final Four for us. But this is what I remember most: when her top-of-the-key three went in, it was almost as if time stood still. I remember looking around the Ford Center arena, where all the people seemed to be in syrupy slow motion. They tell me the noise was deafening, and yet it sounded muffled to me. I took in the panoramic view and realized what we had become: we'd become our freshman phenom. The whole place was splashing about in Whit's passion. That was her modus operandi. She was a spreader of joy.

Then, unfortunately, the story went off line.

The following November, on a random fastbreak as Whit loped down the right lane of the court, she received a run-of-the-mill outlet pass and crumbled to the floor in a heap. Her shrill cry needed no explanation. She clutched her knee toward her chest, and we didn't need a doctor to tell us that her journey was taking a turn.

She slogged through that sophomore year. She was a captain, and she tried like crazy to be a great one. She dove into rehab. She poured her heart into her team. But she also wrestled. As we won and lost and stretched and grew, she struggled to feel where she fit. And she was constantly at war with her mind. Our team locked arms and refused to be anything less than fabulous, yet with every win, Whit's imprisoned competitor's heart flailed. She never wanted us to not be great, but our gains magnified her loss. And the thing that so defined her flickered, hidden from view.

We wound up back at the Final Four. Whitney wept the entire time. Without the ability to play the game, she groped like a person trapped in the dark; she could not find her joy. And when it was over, she beat herself up for all that she wanted to be and was not. I have never seen a kid so willing to name her own warts. She was so determined to grow.

After a successful rehab, a summer of swelling and tweaking and a subsequent surgery to microfracture her bones and clean up the mess, Whit made her way back to the court, though she never really returned to her champion's stride. She made plays and competed, but every day she hurt, and every single thing seemed to be way harder than it should have been. Our season ended in the NCAA tournament at the round of 16, and it seemed like Whit's spirit was left dangling while her body was being held together with Scotch Tape.

In Whit's fourth year—her junior season due to the medical red-shirt—we earned ourselves a six seed in the NCAA tournament, where we hosted St. John's University on our home floor in the opening round. But this foray into the post-season held surprises of its own. The week of the game, one of our players came down with a stomach virus, and teammates began to fall like dominoes. By week's end, our entire team and staff were deathly ill from the virus that ran through our facility like a plague. I had never before seen a bug so rampant and severe. We all did the best we could, playing and coaching dehydrated, depleted, and desperate. We had pre-game IV's and halftime drips. Players subbed out of the game and raced up the tunnel to the bathroom from the opening tip to the buzzer at the end. We called substitution timeouts just to keep five people on the floor. All of our players were pale and gaunt, their energy void palpable. But Whit's bravery eclipsed us all. She and I were among the last to get ill, so our bouts were at their worst at game time. I could scarcely sit upright in the chair; to this day I have no idea how she played. But she did. For forty minutes. And when the buzzer blew and we didn't have enough points to fight on, Whit's lifeless body lay spent in our locker room, a true athlete's carcass with her pounding heart still out on the floor.

From where we all stood then, it just seemed so unfair.

Some people are really good when asked to adorn something, but not so much so when asked to be the something that gets adorned. When accessorizing is needed, they can reflect and add color; they can make a thing work. But being the core? That's another thing entirely. In all of Whitney's seasons, as the winds and waves howled around her, she was always the core. She was so good at it, she made it look easy. Because she did what she did, her teammates were able to revel in their roles. They could hang on, tag along… they could even ride along sometimes, because Whit would eventually get them where they wanted to go. It wore on her, though she would never in a million years admit it. But it also made her insides grow so stout you could bounce a penny off her gut. The will with which she competed propelled us. Her senior year would be the stuff of legend—she and everyone around her just knew it. Her teammates hitched their wagons to her star, and away we went.

Whit's final season began with one of her fellow seniors being sidelined with a career-ending back injury. A couple of months into preseason, another teammate starter blew her Achilles tendon. After returning from a Thanksgiving tournament in which she had been outstanding, our freshman point guard tore her ACL. All of a sudden, we were down to nine. We couldn't even practice five on five. I remember aching for every kid—grieving, actually—as each particular situation came laced with demons all its own. And I came completely undone for Whit. I felt like she deserved better. I wanted her to ride off on a white horse. I wanted her to wear the crown. If ever there were a kid who had earned it, she had. And I felt like with every injury, our chances for a return to the Final Four dwindled. It got harder and harder to take.

The two days after our team's third season-ending injury were disjointed. We all tried to act as if nothing had changed, but we all knew so much had. We absorbed and forged on, but we were undeniably shaken, and the emotional toll was obvious in our ensuing performance. We sputtered against a scrappy "we've got nothing to lose" North Texas team, looking like a squad that was very well aware of how much we had already lost.

We had no idea.

With 1:50 remaining in the first half, Whitney planted her feet to take a jumpshot in transition, and our world stopped on a dime.

When a knee goes, you know it, especially when it's the second time. You don't need a trainer to yank on it or an MRI film for proof. I knew. Whitney knew. Every person in the building knew. I will never forget the heaviness of that air. When they carried Whit off the court to a thunderous standing ovation, I clapped, too, but I could not feel my hands. I watched Morgan guard with tears rolling down her face. I shook my head as Jo tried to shoot before she completely caught the ball. I screamed at Maddie, Lyns, and KK, our three already-injured reserves, to lift their buried heads and be with us! But all any of us wanted was for halftime to come so we could run out of the gym and find some air to breathe.

In the locker room, I circled the stools and told our guys to get through the next twenty minutes, to just find a way to function, and to win for Whit. That's what she would want more than anything. We would figure the rest of it out later. With bleeding insides, that's exactly what they did. But when the game was over, we knew we had a season to complete, and we had to find a way to do it without Whitney dragging us all along. The forecast was dark, and everybody was scared. I just remember being numb.

During the days ahead, I had to keep telling myself what I had always told my players: you can't ask why a bad thing happens unless you're willing to ask why all the good things happen, too. I was able to avoid the pitfalls of the questioning cavern of my belly, but I lived every second of every day two swallows away from a cry. One of the best to ever come through our program was done. She wouldn't play again. It seemed unfathomable that she would be denied her joy and her teammates would be robbed of her influence.

I've never seen an athlete mourn the end of her playing days the way Whitney did. Sorrow rattled her bones. And then she hobbled back into our gym, dove into the souls of her teammates, and refused to go away.

She brought with her the joy she had discovered while crawling around in the dark, the kind that no longer had to be plugged into her ability to perform. Her daily diligence was the kind of thing that took your breath away. She steeled us together with her resolve, and we grew muscles where we'd never had them before. She and her fellow injured teammates created a joy-wrapped cocoon that kept us buoyed with a lifeline of courage, faith, and tenacity—a seemingly endless supply from which we could freely draw.

If a leader's primary job is to be a dealer in hope, Whitney Hand was a leader of rare air. When the second knee blew, she could have disappeared. No one would have blamed her; she had paid more than her share of dues. But cutting and running was not in her DNA. So she showed up, open wounds and all, day after day after day after day, and every fiber of her being was in the middle of the fray.

As a result, our bruised and battered squad limped all the way to the NCAA round of 16.

When the year was over, Whit made and laminated a sign that hung for years in her old locker. It read in part, "To the future owner of this locker: (1) Put up pictures (2) Clean up your crap (3) Smile a LOT…(10) You play at the best place on earth. Don't take it for granted."

Her career was not at all as she or any of us imagined it would be, but it could be argued that it was better in all sorts of unseen ways. I maintain that Whitney's headline trait was her diligence: "careful and persistent work or effort." It's just so darn rare. But her diligence was wrapped in happy—the kind of joy-laced ribbon that they don't sell in stores—and that's what made her so impactful. She got all over you whether you wanted her to or not. And you were better because she did.

Some things just don't fit on stat lines or have columns in record books. Whitney Hand's influence could never be housed on a page. The seeds just scattered, and rooted in all kinds of places, changing the landscape as they grew.

THE PROTECTOR

WE WINED AND DINED her in the Wendy's at the Student Union. Her mother told us she had been offered a scholarship by almost every single Big 12 institution, and that a number of the teams had offered her the keys to their kingdom. I told both her and her mother that we were offering a scholarship as well, and that I'd love the chance to coach her, but that she'd have to earn any playing time she got and nothing was guaranteed. We showed her our beautiful campus first, our lousy locker room last, and told her if she wanted to be a part of building something special she should call us once she got home.

Caton Hill left and drove home to Ada, Oklahoma. The next morning, she called while I was getting ready for work. She wanted to make a difference. She was headed to Oklahoma. She'd be joining us in the fall.

For four years, Caton was a central cog in our Big Red Machine. She was an undersized post/power forward who pushed big girls off the block and outfoxed all the foxes she couldn't outrun. She was a bossy, emotional player who rarely forgot where to go or what to do. If the scout said, "Send this player left," then send her left she did.

And if you were on her team, she expected you to know and do the same. She had that iron will in her marrow, the rarified kind that more often than not made her better than she was.

Caton played basketball with her gut, a personal sense of purpose, and an edgy toughness all balled up in one. That gut led us to the National Championship game in 2002. It led her to medical school in 2004. In 2009, she followed it to Afghanistan, where she lived in tents and operated on pilots, serving her country during the war.

From day one, Caton Hill wanted to be a doctor. Her father and her uncle served in the United States Army, so when she combined her passion for medicine with an enlistment, I was not surprised. She came in first in sharpshooting at basic training camp, and we all giggled and rolled our eyes. Of course she did! And when she wrestled with the decisions of medical specialty by tapping on the glass ceiling of alpha-male-dominated orthopedics, we all cheered her on, confident that if she wanted to break into the club, she could. Since the first day I met her, I have known one thing: there is very little Caton Hill cannot do.

As an athlete, however, Caton was somewhat limited. She shot the basketball with old-school form from the perimeter, and her finishes around the rim, while effective, were never textbook pretty. We liked to say she was "vertically challenged," and yet at 6' 0" (on a good day), there wasn't a rebound she couldn't pull down. Her "want to" was off the charts.

As I spoke with Caton in the weeks and days leading up to her deployment, I could tell that she was keenly aware of the magnitude of her assignment. She was what the Army calls a flight doctor. Her charge was to keep our fighting pilots healthy. In essence, she protected them so they could protect us.

My slow, vertically challenged, undersized center lived in a tent in the desert where she wore camo and vests that weighed around fifty pounds while the temperatures hovered in the 100s. She heard gunfire. She watched people die. She saw poverty, affliction, cowardice, and brutality the likes of which those of us here in America cannot comprehend. These are the spoils you're left with when you sign up to protect and serve.

Caton said to me on the phone before she left for Afghanistan that college basketball had been hard, even in light of her military training. And in a strange sort of way I felt proud that maybe we— her teammates, her coaches, and her competition—had played some small role in helping to prepare her to be where she was, doing what she was doing—being brave and true and purposeful, making that difference she always felt compelled to make.

For all the things Caton was on the basketball floor, the one thing she was NOT defines her in my mind. You see, ironically, Caton could never take a charge. She would take a stand in the path of an oncoming offensive player in an attempt to draw a foul, but at the moment of contact, she could not take the fall. The offensive player would be the one who went flying and Caton would be charged with a foul. Every time. She would try in practice. She would try in games. She would try after practice when she thought no one was looking. She would plant her feet and beg teammates to plow through her, but she just never could make herself fall down. It was ironic because she was the consummate teammate. She'd set a screen that would rattle your brain if you dared foul or even appeared to trouble one of her guards. She would rotate on defense and bail you out time after time after time if you couldn't take care of your assignment and you needed help getting out of a jam. But she couldn't take a charge to save her life.

And I think I finally understand why. Taking a charge went against everything Caton Hill believed and stood for internally: You do not fall down. When hit, you do not move. You are the wall. Falling is for the other guy.

Caton was a protector, a guardian, a player whose toughness was her calling card even though she was intricately skilled. As much as anyone I've ever coached, Caton's game mirrored the way her insides were wound. She was not a player who needed to be wooed, and she didn't need an easy road. What Caton wanted and needed was a challenge—and someone to take care of, someone to serve. That's who she was on and off the court. The same person wearing different uniforms, standing firmly planted, refusing to take the fall.

OUR CANADIAN STAR

WE CALLED HER SKIPPY. I can't remember exactly when we started or why. She always kind of bounced around on her toes, but there has to be more to it than that.

We found Stacey Dales in a random gym in Scarborough, Canada. (Home of Jim Carey, but he's the second-best thing to come out of there, if you're asking me.) My assistant coach had gone there to watch a point guard whom we'd seen on film but I knew wasn't good enough to help us win. My coach asked if she could go watch her anyway—you never know, she said—we might see something in person that the film couldn't convey. We needed a point guard desperately, and I didn't think this kid was the answer, but I gave approval for my assistant to go. Perhaps a miracle was hiding in the frozen tundra. We were certainly in need of one.

My colleague called breathlessly the following day.

"I've found our savior," she said. I asked her if she was drunk.

She laughed and admitted she'd like to be, but instead she was at a gym. Not the gym she'd flown there to go to; she'd watched the player she went to see and left disappointed, feeling like she had wasted too much money and too much time. But someone told her about some games being played at a spot down the road, so she stopped in there, figuring she had nothing to lose. She had absolutely no clue what she was about to have a chance to gain.

That's how we found our needle in a haystack, the one and only Stacey Dales.

I could hear it in my assistant's voice. She told me what she saw and what she felt, but she didn't even know the kid's name. I told her to stay and dig for details. Then I crossed my fingers and my toes and put a rally cap on just in case. We'd need all the good vibes we could gather, if we wanted to pull this one off.

A week later, I flew to Brockville, Ontario, to see our Canadian prize.

Stacey was the point guard who jumped center. Weird. Unlikely. But I wanted to put her in my suitcase before the opening tip. Never before or since had I seen such unbridled anticipation before the toss of a ball. I can't remember whether or not she won the tip-off, but I won't ever forget the way she looked in pursuit. That's how I knew.

Stacey Dales had *it*. In spades. And I wanted *it* on my team.

The game itself was somewhat brutal. Stace easily had six or seven turnovers in the first quarter alone. But I loved what she saw when she played. She saw plays before they developed, teammates before they were open, and driving lanes to the basket before the defense even parted ways. Some passes were missiles, their intended targets never even aware that they were ones, and some were as soft as clouds, the ball placed in the only sphere of space it could rest in for a teammate's grab-and-go. She ran like a gazelle, skinny legs everywhere, and eyes all over the gym.

Stacey Dales was dynamite in a long, tall package, and I wanted to coach her so badly I could hardly breathe. When I look back in retrospect, it still feels so unlikely. Before our home visit, she grabbed a globe from the top of her closet to see where Oklahoma even was. Getting her was a bit like winning the lottery, and though we worked hard to make it happen, it felt like we opened the hopper and somehow she pulled out our name.

We had lousy dorms and a worse team, but that didn't scare Stacey in the least. She didn't see what was in front of her, only what could be—both on and off the court. Her vision always put her in a superhero lane.

Stace arrived in Oklahoma the following fall carrying her dreams and all of ours, too, even if she didn't realize it at the time. She was passion personified, all bouncy and big-eyed and hungry for whatever anyone could dish out. She thought she was better than she was, yet had no idea how good she could be. I found that charisma-wrapped dichotomy more fun than a bag of Legos on Christmas morning. She came daily to the gym like a baby bird with her mouth open, begging to be fed. She had places to go and she wanted all the fuel we could give her. In that way, she was a coach's dream.

In some other ways, maybe not so much.

Stacey was high strung and moody and so homesick I thought she was going to have to be hospitalized. Every evening when the sun went down it took her heart right with it, so nights were filled with long phone calls to Canada and lots and lots of tears. We took turns taking her for ice cream and giving her rides to the gym to shoot.

We did everything we could think of to distract her, but the start of the season was the only thing that anchored her in this foreign place so far from everything she knew. With each rip of the calendar's page, her gait grew lighter and her sadness less intense. She couldn't wait to play her first game. And we couldn't wait to watch her. We went to San Antonio, Texas for our season opener. We were poised to take the world by storm.

My pregame speech came straight from a movie. I gave 'em the "Win one for the Gipper" speech, almost verbatim from the Hollywood film *Rudy*, while standing on a table spewing saliva just like him as best I could. Our players ran out of the locker room, their feet barely touching the ground. Then they giggled and strutted their way through warm-ups like they were cranking a jack-in-the-box. They knew what nobody else was aware of: a superstar was about to pop out and shock the world.

Unfortunately, the plot was about to twist.

We won the tip, ran a back screen for Stace, and threw her an alley-oop in the perfect spot, just two feet to the right of the rim. Three long strides and a take-off later, she was in a wad on the floor, clutching her left knee. It was like watching the too-short Challenger spaceflight: exuberance, anticipation, awe for what was about to be, followed by a lift off that went very, very wrong right before our eyes.

Stacey's ACL was torn. Her season was done. Our dream machine pushed pause.

That moment set the stage for Stace, though she couldn't feel it at the time. It gave her a season she hadn't expected and didn't know she needed. A season to get stronger, to grow some sinew on the inside, to sit and watch and learn the game.

Sitting out starved her for competition, so she sought out battles wherever she could find them, about any and everything. She yearned to spar, so she did—with rehab, with theories presented in her classes, with people who had different opinions, with the demons in her head—all the while wearing her passion like a prizefighter's silky robe.

Stace built her gears while she was living on the side. Internal capacity comes before skill and scope, and she had to see the progression required to get from here to there. Once she understood it, she could construct a system that would allow her to impact a game beyond what she did with the ball. The purview from the sideline taught her how much more she could do.

In the fall of 1998, Stacey Dales finally made her re-debut. Fans got swooped up in her bravado, riding the wave of all she promised, relishing the potential of *wow* when the ball was in her hands. Without question, her performance did not disappoint. It became evident very quickly that Stacey Dales was worth the wait.

We coaches were like cartoonists, and she was the animation director. We'd sketch the pictures, she would bring them to life. I was hard-pressed to draw up anything she couldn't make happen. Her artistry was a lethal combination of what she did and the adept, stylistic way with which she did it.

But it was her teammates who really got rich. If you could run, Stace made you faster. If you could finish, she'd put the ball right where you needed it to be. If you could rebound, she'd cash it in for fast money. She was Midas with an orange leather ball. And that was just the outside stuff.

Where Stace really excelled was in the way she made everybody involved in the game *feel*. She was vitamin D for the people on her team. She was funny (like side-stitch funny) and self-deprecating and smart. She was intuitive, observant, and unabashedly bold. She'd wrap her long skinny arm around some shoulders and put her long skinny foot up others' butts, having an innate sense of which was required at the time.

And moxie oozed from her pores with her sweat.

We used to say that we began most games ahead of the competition by ten. Opposing coaches sat on the bench and just watched her warm up as their teams tried nervously to pretend she wasn't there. My assistant coaches loved watching pregame because Stacey started winning then, while most players had no idea the game was even on.

Stacey spread her wings as a point guard, as an athlete, and as a leader, and she grew to fill them every year. She just got better and better and better, and so did we. By the time she was a junior, we'd built a program. By her senior year, we had ourselves a squad.

Our team wasn't deep and we weren't very big, but we were skilled and we were smart and everybody just kind of seemed to know where everybody else was going to be on the court. Controlled chaos led by the Canadian diamond who'd allowed herself to be honed. It was basketball the way it was meant to be played.

In the spring of that year, our Stacey-Dales-driven team took the floor in San Antonio at the Alamodome to compete in the Final Four. We were in the same city of Stacey's inauspicious beginnings five years earlier; we'd come full circle. There was, no doubt, some destiny involved.

The night before the first-round game, we participated in the NCAA's traditional Salute Dinner. This was a magnificent, formal evening hosted by the Final Four city, and San Antonio did it up right! Part of the program was a live roast featuring each of the four head coaches and a player from each team. Stacey was my sidekick on the stage, and she ran away with the crowd. She did imitations of me, a funny thumbnail sketch of our team, and a little Saturday Night Live re-enactment of "Sally O'Malley" as an encore. She was as natural there as she was on the court. The Oklahoma Sooners won the local fan base and Stacey Dales stole the show.

In the national semi-final game, we broke away from Duke with 7:40 to go in the second half. We hit a three-point shot in transition, called time-out to make a defensive substitution, and the run was on. We were headed to compete in the final game of the year.

When the game was over, we stood at half court in front of 29,000 fans—Stacey Dales and I—with Doris Burke, the ESPN sideline reporter, and we tried to answer questions about the one game we had left to play. Dales had her arm draped around me, towering above me even though I had on four-inch heels, and we could scarcely hear the questions over the roar of the crowd.

"Boomer," one side screamed.

"Sooner," the other side thundered back.

Back and forth it went, as if we were at Owen Field in Norman on a Saturday afternoon in the fall. Standing there with this kid on that court in that space was about as good as it gets this side of the pearly gates.

Stace worked the camera and the crowd and then skipped off, as she was apt to do. Off to the locker room to keep our crew on task, because as happy as she was, she knew we weren't finished. We hadn't yet done what we had come to do.

Those were Stacey's best moments. The big ones. She could rise to any occasion, flip the switch, and win the room. She could will a shift in momentum, ride a wave to the point of no return, and if you put the ball in her hand when the game was on the line, she would make the play. She had gears that most couldn't find and wouldn't know what to do with if they did.

Unfortunately, Stacey's collegiate basketball story lacked a fairytale ending. She fouled out of the championship game with just under two minutes remaining, and though we gave a valiant effort, the spoils went to the other team.

Stacey Dales, however, had become a star. A gambler who bet on us in the beginning, but bet on herself by choosing us, too. Her ace was always her confidence. She believed devoutly in where she could go and what she could do and who she could be. I guess she always sort of knew—from the time she pulled down her globe from the top of her closet when we called to recruit her and she wondered where Oklahoma was—that her trajectory would be up to her. So she set her eyes on the skies and made herself a place there, leaving a trail for future dreamers who'd like to end up there, too.

MASTER OF THE MARGINS

SHANNON SELMON SHOULD get a prize. She had to listen to my raspy voice and endure my soapbox sermons for seven years, and that's more than plenty for anyone. I coached her for three years in high school because she was good enough to play on the varsity team when she was just in the ninth grade. Then, as she entered her senior year of high school, I left for the University of Oklahoma, and as soon as she graduated, I asked her to come, too. She was the daughter of an Oklahoma football legend. Dewey is her dad, one of the super trio of Selmon Brothers who demonized backfields throughout their gridiron careers at Owen Field in Norman, Oklahoma. That part was a bonus.

Shannon was a scrappy undersized post player who just knew how to win. She was never the best player on any of our teams, but she made every team she played on better. Shannon was a dyed-in-the-wool competitor. She was Churchill's quintessential grinner as she fought.

Some players love to score points and some are enamored with blocking shots, but loose balls were Shannon's joy. She went after them like a puppy with oversized feet and a treat on the line. And when she got them, usually she came up smiling. Excelling there in the margins of the game, she separated herself from the pack.

The Selmon family is a family of believers. Their faith is a thread sewn devoutly throughout the community of Norman and the entire state of Oklahoma. Shannon's mom, Kathryn, is a pillar at Food and Shelter for Friends, so all six of her kids formed load-bearing walls there, too. They've served thousands of folks who were hungry or lost or simply in between their own becoming over the years. Service is part of the Selmon DNA.

And that's how Shannon played. Not so much like a waitress, because she couldn't pass with pizzazz. But more like the point man, because she would make the way. She was the lead recon guy... the one sticking her foot inside the door, hugging the corner as she went to make sure the way was safe for everyone to go in. She assessed everything—the stuff available to the naked eye as well as all the stuff that wasn't. The lay of the land was always Shannon Selmon's domain.

That's how she played for sure, but that's also how she lived.

In 2005, the Selmon family created the Shine Foundation, a nonprofit organization established to assist impoverished children. One of their first targets of influence was Gbarnga, Liberia. Shannon's sister, Lauren, was working there co-managing the development of Rainbow Town, an orphanage in the civil-war-torn country. In the summer of that year, Shannon, her brother Zac, the rest of their family, and a small collection of other University of Oklahoma athletes made the trek across the water to make a difference. They took balls and Bibles and the work ethic pulsing through each of their veins to children in a different world with other-worldly needs.

This little Oklahoma tribe went to Africa to teach a sports camp while building a school. They succeeded at both. And in giving all they had, they doubled in size. The love they took with them multiplied as hollow-eyed children were bathed in it and boomeranged it back to them tenfold. Agape spilled out everywhere. The Selmons brought it back in jars without lids.

But let me back up.

When Shannon came to Oklahoma in 1998 to help us construct a program, the foundation had been poured but the walls were still being erected. She quickly became the foreman, driving nails without tire. It's funny—she never played very much (averaging roughly ten minutes a game throughout her career), but she was integral. I want to type that word like David Gray sings *"definite"* in "My Oh My." She was *integral*. It needs intonation only a spoken word can convey just to begin to justify the weight it carries.

In 2000, we hosted the much-ballyhooed Connecticut Huskies at the Lloyd Noble Center on the campus of the University of Oklahoma. I had talked Geno, UCONN's head coach, into scheduling the game because we needed them to help us grow. They were a circus, so when they came to town, people followed. We were trying to gain traction— find some relevance—and we desperately needed a reason for people to come to the arena to watch us play. Connecticut was our scent to get them in the door. Once we got them there, we could win their hearts. I knew we could. We just had to give people a reason to show up.

December 29, 1999, was D-Day. Pre-sale tickets had set records, but in complete transparency, that didn't mean too much because the bar was so low. On game day, I kept getting updates from our Senior Women's Administrator about the sales tick. She couldn't believe what was happening as people just continued to buy.

At 6:20 p.m., we did what we always did before games: our team warmed up. I stayed inside the locker room as tradition held, walking circles in that space. Our team room was on the second floor of the arena. Players ran up the tunnel, up eight stairs, then through the door to a stairwell that housed two flights of twenty. Then they ran about fifty yards, and the Oklahoma Women's Basketball locker room was the last door on the right. You could not make that up.

By 6:45 p.m., I could hear my team making their way back up from the court. Shannon Selmon was the first to round the corner. Her brown eyes the size of saucers, breathless from both the journey up the stairs and the idea of history being made, she said in a dramatic staccato of gulping air, "Coach Coale!" ... "You have built it" ... "And they have come!!" The words and how she said them are imprinted in my brain.

And it was perfect for our air. I laughed, watching them revel in it as they giggled at the thought of an arena full of people watching them play. So there was no room left in which to worry about the opponent we'd be sparring with—a concoction mixed perfectly for our best chance of success. We ran out of the tunnel to play that night tethered only by our Nikes to the court.

10,713 people watched us play.

UCONN beat us pretty soundly in the first half, but we fought back in the second, playing them straight up. In the end we lost by sixteen. But little had ever mattered less.

We had hooked some hearts.

We sent out homemade postcards that had a picture of the jam-packed arena on the front and a thank you note from me on the back to every ticket holder we had contact information for in attendance. Someone took a picture of the "sold out" sign on the front of the Lloyd Noble Center door. After December 29, 1999, nothing would ever be the same.

Shannon's faith-to-fruition synopsis of the night was foreshadowing for what would lie ahead. In April of 2002, when we marched into the Alamodome in San Antonio to play in the national championship semi-final game, Shannon battened down the hatches and ran flanker as Stacey Dales and Co. headlined our attack. Our starting five were nasty good. Our sixth player was a freshman (a.k.a. future star) named Dionnah Jackson, and our seventh was Shannon Selmon. We were locked and loaded, entering the arena in a tanker fueled by exponential belief.

With a little less than eight minutes to play in the semi-final game versus Duke, I inserted Shannon into the game. Duke had gone to their post player, Iciss Tillis (is that a great name or what!), on four consecutive trips. She was taller than us, she had arms that stretched for days, and she was crazy skilled, so the strategy was a good one. We stood behind her with our hands outstretched but couldn't eclipse her view. The ball just kept going in.

On a rare miss, we rebounded it and took off toward our goal. I had needed to call a time out for several possessions, but I kept holding off, waiting for the right moment. So when Caton Hill nailed a three in transition to put us up three, I knew it was time. We needed to adjust our defensive strategy: we had to front the post. And nobody did that better than Shannon—she was so good at following a plan. So I sent her to the table and she scooted into the game, where she fronted Iciss at the block just like we told her. Duke tried lobbing, and they threw it out of bounds. They tried bouncing it around Shannon, but she tipped it away. Our team took Duke's miscues and turned them into Oklahoma points. We won the game 86–71. Two days later we would play for the National Championship. Shannon Selmon had contributed eight of the most important minutes of our year.

She did her difference-making in the margins. She was the maestro of the pauses—the ones most people chose not to pay attention to—the ones that connected the notes.

Shannon spoke to my teams regularly in the following years, often retelling a story from her time in Liberia shortly after she finished college and her basketball career was done. The story is about Ma Feeta, the woman from Liberia who is the anchor of the Rainbow Town orphanage.

Ma Feeta took in ninety-six children from the bush because a soldier had said to her, "Take the children or you will die." She had fallen into an ambush while running from the war, and she didn't see any children anywhere, but when the guy said it three times, she figured somebody other than him was talking. So she followed him into the bush. And there she found them. All ninety-six of all ages, shoeless, hungry, and scared.

Ma Feeta tied the children to each other by their shirttails and led them away from the fighting, sometimes for days without food. By the time Shannon's sister, Lauren, met Ma Feeta, over 200 children were in her care. She didn't lose any of the original ninety-six. Not one. As a matter of fact, she just kept picking up more. It was the story of the loaves and fishes in an upside-down-backward kind of way.

Ma Feeta was a heavy lifter. Shannon valued how she carried her load. That's why she shared Ma's story when she spoke.

Another Shine Foundation story that Shannon shared is about Steven, her most valuable player from the school build in 2005. Steven was a local Liberian hired to shuttle the water between two hills— from the bottom of the lowest to the top of the highest. The water was necessary for making the bricks, but it was only available at the bottom. The building was going up at the top, and the only way to get the water where it was needed was by hand. Steven's hands were paid the equivalent of one US dollar for every day of getting it there. His gratitude without hesitation is what captured Shannon's heart.

She says, "He just kept saying, 'I thank God. I thank God. I thank God.' With a smile that dwarfed his face." She says Steven taught her that gut-generated gratitude comes swiftly and ferociously. And that it's impossible to contain.

What Shannon saw in Ma Feeta and in Steven, ironically, is what we all see in her. It's exactly what made her *integral* to all that we were and did. Shannon owned the margins as a student-athlete. She ran the locker room, glued together the game plans, and served the heroes as they starred. She carried whatever load was asked of her valiantly, her signature always her see-through heart.

And she is all that still. As a mother and a daughter and a sister and a friend, she is part Ma Feeta, part Steven, part the Selmons, and all God's. She collects the good that she encounters and she knows exactly what to do with it. She passes it on.

MS. MATTER-OF-FACT

SHE IS FAMOUS FOR *THE SLOOP.* That's the term I coined for her atypical delivery of the basketball. She never really shot it, and she was always leaning one way or the other when it left her hand, so it just seemed to slide from her care to the rim.

Unorthodox. That's the word that always comes to mind when I think of Jamie shooting the basketball. Actually, that's the word that comes to mind when I think about her play in general. But you could never argue with what she got done.

In 2002, Jamie Talbert anchored our offense as a 6' 0" post player (though the media guide lied and listed her at 6' 2") whose vertical barely allowed light to shine under her shoes. She was the perfect foil for a backcourt high in talent and in personality. Jamie was no-excuses vanilla, Ms. Matter-of-Fact. And she was a competitor of extraordinary degree.

I'm ashamed to this day to say that I never really recruited her. We were recruiting the point guard on her junior college team, as well as a young foreign kid, but the last thing we needed was another undersized post player. I didn't even know who Jamie Talbert was in 2000. But I wasn't stupid. On my third trip to Seward County Community College, I told her coach, Jim Littell, that he had one heck of a team but #45 was his team's heartbeat. She's who won his games. He said, "You think I don't know that? Why don't you sign HER?"

I thought that was a splendid idea.

So I did. And that was that. Two years later she helped carry the tattered American flag from the 9/11 site onto the playing surface at San Antonio's Alamodome. That night in the national championship game, she guarded the ever-rotating huge and talented post cadre for arguably the best women's basketball team ever assembled from the University of Connecticut. No one had a higher order in that title game than Tal. Though our team came up a bit short in the end, she swung and swung and swung, leaving the Alamodome valiantly—just like she entered it. Consistency had always been her ace.

In the spring of 2002, I watched Jamie graduate from the University of Oklahoma with a degree in microbiology. In the summer of 2004, I watched her walk down the aisle to trade in her maiden name for one that I still fail to use when referring to her. (Though her last name now is Wyrick, to me she will always be Tal.) And in the fall of 2005, I watched her sit in a pleather recliner while chemo was fed into her veins. She was a twenty-five-year-old physical therapy student who wrestled cancer in her spare time. Guarding Tamika, Swin, and Asia—Connecticut's golden triumvirate—was nothing compared to this.

I sensed an irritation in Tal during her treatment, though not necessarily any fear. She was a medical student at the time, so she knew more than enough to be afraid. But she didn't seem to be that as much as she was annoyed. Her hair was gone, but the bandana she wore looked so natural I kept forgetting her hair was in a box somewhere. As the red devil dripped, we talked about how much she missed playing basketball games and how much she didn't miss getting her body conditioned to play. She said it was just the stuff teammates do together—all the "times"—that you really crave once basketball is gone. As she sat there covered in a light blanket fighting the satanic disease called cancer, confidence was still her crowning glory, as it had always been. And *grace* was the word that kept swirling around and around in my mind.

Tal would kill me if I wrote a story about her. That has so never been her way. So I want to write about what she was a part of. She always got *team* in the truest sense.

A couple of months into the chemotherapy, Jamie's former teammates came by the office to ask if we, the coaches and current team, were interested in pitching in. They were getting her a wig. A real one. One she could swim and shower in, one she could style and put up in a ponytail. One she could get sweaty and messed up— an athlete's crown as much as possible like the one God gave her himself over twenty years ago. And au naturel items like real hair wigs don't come cheap. Tal's teammates from all over were sending money. I could sense from the three who came calling that this was a necessary mission for them. They were fighters, all of them. They were workers who needed to do. So from the crevices of law school and medical school and within the pursuit of master's degrees and the teaching of America's youth, the group that put Oklahoma Women's Basketball on the national map got busy and they got our girl a wig.

Their knowledge of it all was nothing short of amazing. They knew the problem with synthetic ones—it seems to have a lot to do with the part—and they knew the benefits of finding ones sewed by hand, using real hair—it seemed to have a lot to do with the hairline and the way it was sewn in. This group was always so good at the art of detail. Steph Simon, forever the team organizer, told me that every one of our current players at the time laid down their monthly scholarship travel money for Tal's new hair. Several had never met her. Most only knew her as a loyal alumnus who sat courtside for home games sometimes, or as the subject of my sermons about effort and concentration and wringing your potential dry. Money came in checks large and small, and prayers wafted from everywhere. Family takes care of family. That's just the way it is.

It was almost as if the infantry had lined up to look this demon in the eye. When you picked on Jamie Talbert, you picked on all of us. And we do not go quietly, we wanted that disease to know. Tal always had Stacy Dales's back when Dales got too fired up and overran a passing lane. She always had the off-side board covered when Roz's three bounced a little long. You could count on her going to the dots every time Caufield drove baseline, and if Tal got fouled in the act of shooting, the free throw was going in. Some things you just learn to know. Des and Caton and Jen and Kate and Steph and Stace... their arms locked, wove in and out with all of us who were bound and determined to protect the "sloop."

One day you're jogging with your dog, and the next day forever is tomorrow and nothing looks the same. Except for the people in your foxhole. They never go away.

THE GOLD BALL

"BE CAREFUL WHAT YOU ASK FOR, you just might get it," the back of the T-shirt said. Our student body printed them up, and they sold like hotcakes. Kids bought them. Parents bought them. Fans bought them. Our biggest rival had said they wanted to play us in the playoffs. They got us—and we won by thirty. Hence the T-shirts. But then, when the whole town descended on Tulsa's Mabee Center—the arena where the Oklahoma high school state tournament was played—wearing the cocky mantra for our state semi-final rematch, the ball went square and we were the ones that got it. We were supposed to give it. Final score: Choctaw 40, Norman 37. It wasn't pretty—the game or the aftermath. I will never as long as I live forget the hollow sorrow of that group of girls.

Our squad regrouped that spring. We locked arms and attacked summer league with a vengeance. Our talented crew destroyed everyone in our path without ever seeming to try very hard to do it. Our jaws were set. There wasn't ever much celebrating when we won, though. We just dove in, sort of surgically wiped a team out, and then went on our way in search of another means of purging.

Summer gave way to fall and our posturing squad tiptoed into preseason workouts, faking out everyone in sight. (Except, of course, ourselves.) A few weeks in, I asked my assistant coach what he thought was wrong.

He said, "What are you talking about?"

And I told him, "Something's not right. Something's missing."

He said, "It's a long time until March, Coach. They know the part that matters. Give them time."

So I did. Two weeks was an eternity for me. That's how long it took until my dam just burst.

One day I blew the whistle in the middle of practice, sending everyone to the locker room. They hadn't messed up a drill; they hadn't loafed; no one had talked back. Everything was good, but nothing was right. I couldn't stand the incongruity of it all. Into the locker room they filed, a bunch of scabbed-over dreamers who were scared to death that the proverbial pot at the end of the rainbow had a hole in it. The silence in that concrete den was deafening.

"What's the deal?" I said to the top of fifteen heads whose eyes were very interested in the floor beneath them. Pregnant pause. "Somebody want to tell me what's going on?" Surprise to none: the brazen summer goddesses had gone mute. They had no opinions. No one shuffled their feet, no one hemmed or hawed—my cocky bunch scarcely even breathed. And so I asked, through fear so thick you would need a machete to carve your way out of it, "What is it you are afraid of?" And fifteen sets of eyes the size of silver dollars rose to look at me as if I'd found the holy grail.

"Let me guess," I said, enjoying the perspective that a summer of soul-searching had afforded me. "You are scared to go all in again. You are afraid to go after this thing with all of your being, like you did before, because you have no guarantees that you can make it happen and you don't ever want to feel like you felt last spring." Bingo. Fifteen heads nodded in unison, and I ached for their terror. I shared it to a degree, but it was my job to grab this moment, the "teachable one" that comes when it's ready but rarely when you are.

I told them in a quivering voice of faith that things of real value never come with a guarantee. I told them we were talented enough that we might be able to go through the motions and win the whole darn thing. That was a fact. But I also told them that selling out and pursuing it with all of our being promises us nothing in return. Then I told them what I prayed was true. "Life gives you no guarantees. But I know one thing: if you sell out and lose, it will mean more to you than if you go through the motions and win. It's not about what you get at the end. It's about how you choose to live the pursuit." Growing bold from my own admonition, I added, "I have news for you. I only know one way to go about a thing, and that's full out. So if you want to tiptoe hopefully toward an end, you're going to have to do it without me." And I left that tomb of a locker room to the fifteen sets of silver-dollar-eyes staring at the fork in the road.

The next day was frenzied—a typical high school day, by definition—filled with loose ends that had to be chased and tied before I could go to practice. I wrapped up just in time to run through the tiled hallways of the school to our practice in the old south gym.

As I reached down for the old iron handle on the creaky double doors to the gym, my heart was in my throat. I had no idea where the previous day's conversation had taken my team, and I knew I'd have a decision to make for myself if the air in the gym hadn't changed. But when I opened the door, I knew what they'd chosen.

You could smell it. You could taste it. You could hear it. You could feel it. My kids had decided to dive in headfirst. They weren't going to tiptoe around. They weren't going to close their eyes and back down the road. My guys were going for it—no guarantees, no promises, no safety net. They were in, come what may. It was 110 degrees in that sweatbox, but there wasn't one square inch of my body that didn't have a goosebump on it. No other team had a chance come March. I knew that in my bones. It was only September.

Seven months later, our team ran out of the tunnel at the Mabee Center on the campus of Oral Roberts University, the site of the previous season's devastation. We were ushered onto the State Championship stage in grand fashion, with smoke and strobe lights and a booming spot that locked on our team as they lined up along the baseline, holding hands like paper dolls. The bright lights made them appear invincible, but the crocodile tears rolling down their faces made them real. The game announcer introduced each team member and then the starting five, and what I had to say in the huddle that followed made absolutely no difference whatsoever. Our players had long ago gone in headfirst. They'd bound their hearts together without the safety of a guarantee. The game was just the outward expression of the brave decisions already seared in their souls.

We took the floor, and our first defensive stand was the finest I've seen in all my years of coaching. We were *rabid*. Unlike the surgical summer-league squad we had been just months before, we reveled in every single play. I had never seen before, and I've yet to see since, a squad so united in the joy of competition. The poetry of our fight landed us a dominating early lead and a performance that cajoled the opposing coach into utilizing all of her time-outs with twenty-one minutes left to play. And the madness grew from there. We took a twenty-five-point lead into halftime and opened the third quarter with a three from my point guard. The margin never wavered from that point on.

As the game wound down, I had the unique opportunity to take my seniors out one at a time. They left their high-school careers to thunderous applause, tear-stained hugs, and a resilience that is born only from immersion. The powers that be handed us the gold ball at center court, and while I know there were people everywhere, I don't remember any of them. I don't remember the noise and can't recall the handshakes, but I will never forget the joy.

Reporters afterward wanted to talk about redemption and comebacks and the obvious justification we must feel from replacing failure with record-setting success. Our players knew more than the reporters gave them credit for, though. The fulfillment ran much deeper than the "monkey off their back" headline the writers were crafting their stories to fit. Our players showered, I conducted the obligatory media interviews, and we boarded that big yellow bus for home. We were twenty miles outside of Tulsa before we discovered we'd left the trophy behind.

It *so* had never been about what you get at the end.

I kept that T-shirt, the one with the caution label on the back. It is my reminder that we must be bold in our aspirations and willing to put our arms around whatever comes toward us along the way. I wish sometimes that all my teams could learn what that one did. Those fifteen starry-eyed kids know now what it feels like to be a part of a thing where full hearts are thrown in the ring. They will forever recognize halfway—in themselves and those they're linked with—and they'll abhor it, even when they're not sure how to make it change. They will be different employees, different spouses, different parents, and better friends because of what they learned together as they slayed dragons of fear on a ninety-four-foot-long hardwood stage.

That raggedy old T-shirt is my badge. It's my "risk to chance reward" trophy that reminds me of the cave that pain can carve and the capacity for joy that can be unleashed to fill it. Be careful what you ask for; you just might get it and then some. I'll keep my fingers crossed that you do.

In memory of my favorite artist, Joe Buben.
Love you Dad

ACKNOWLEDGMENTS

"When you're done you turn things over and get out of the way.
You're not the one who does the work anyway."

—Anne Lamott

SO THIS IS ME MOVING OVER. But before I do, I have lots of people to thank.

To my husband, Dane, thank you for your quiet belief, for giving me the space to always do what I love and for never letting me take any of it, or myself, too seriously. To my daughter, Chandler, for being my creative thinking partner, my technological savior, and my businesswoman role model all in one. I'm so proud of who you are. To my son, Colton, for letting me tell stories about you when you were little and for loving me so hard and so well now that you are big. You've become a marvelous man. To my daughter-in-law, Morgan, we could have searched the whole world over and never found another who fits like you. And, finally, to my granddaughter, Austyn, you hold my heart in your tiny little hands.

I'm grateful to my mom who is a professional spotter–you never see her but she's always there. She and Bob made all the trips, helped with the kids, watched the house, and generally did a lot of the heavy lifting so I could juggle for thirty some odd years. All of that *and* the wind beneath my wings. Talk about a superhero. All that's missing is the cape.

I'm grateful to my brother, Jack, and my best friend, Guy, for being my phone-a-friends on speed dial when I needed a factoid or a metaphor or a pair of eyes to read a thing that I had read to death. Your constant gifts of candor wrapped in "Keep Going!" kept me out of the ditch and off high center. A girl couldn't possibly be tethered by two more incredible guys.

I'm grateful to my Gingerbread Friends—you know who you are—you feed my soul. A special thank you to Jackie for the nudge in the darkness. This project never would have happened without you. Thank you for pushing and championing and generally being the best hound dog anyone could ever have.

My life is what it is because of all the athletes who let me be their coach. Thank you guys for leaving pieces of yourself in me. You taught me more than you will ever know. I am better for my time with you, and I am continually rewarded by your lives.

To the many up-close-and-personal examples of how to coach and lead a team who are not mentioned in this collection of stories —Mary Patton, Elvin Sweeten, Max Dobson, Stephanie Findley, Tony Robinson, Doug Tolin, Jan Ross, Bob Stoops, Kelvin Sampson, Jeff Capel, Lon Kruger—who rubbed off on me in more ways than they will ever know. It was the privilege of a lifetime to watch you work.

To Kay Tangner, thank you for opening the gate to all the angels at Children's Hospital through the years.

To Esther for voicing faith in my writing, for making me believe that these stories could actually become a thing. You'll never know how much your confidence helped to frame my future.

To my meticulous editor, Mary Beth, thank you for calling my attention to chasms without bridges, for nudging me to spit shine, and for always making two plus two equal some number greater than four. You are the whetstone my prose has longed for. Thank you for your pixie dust.

To the people at Scribe—you've got this deal figured out. Thank you for your expertise in all the areas I knew nothing about and for your constant faith in the words. A special thank you to Sophie, my point guard, for always getting the ball where it needed to be, for regularly doling out hope, and for doing what all the great ones do best—being whatever it is your team needed you to be.

And finally, to Anna Quindlen, whom I've never met but feel like I know. Thank you for making everyone who reads you feel that way. When I grow up, I want to write like you.